Time and Tides
on the Western Shore

Albert F. Gray

ALBERT FREDERICK GRAY

An Autobiography

Lovingly dedicated to my father,
GEORGE ALEXANDER GRAY,
Who, my mother taught me to believe,
Was a perfect man;
And whose faults, if he ever had any,
Were never revealed to me.

PREFACE

The author has stood at times gazing with amazement and awe at the vast expanse of the ocean extending before him as far as the eye can see and far beyond the reach of his imagination. There lies the great giant ocean calm and peaceful like a placid lake.

But not for long! With the shrug of a wakening monster the sea moves relentlessly toward the shore with ever enlarging breakers and with ever more deafening roar. On comes the tide. It lays hold on a large ocean liner and lifts it five, ten, twenty or more feet, then quietly lowers it in its berth. What tremendous power; enough to toss about a large ship; yes, power enough to do all the work needed by mankind if it were only harnessed. But the power is not in the ship it is in the ocean tide drawn forward by the strong arms of the moon.

The author thinks of himself as but a piece of drift-wood picked up and tossed forward and upward by the surging tide till, having spent its effort, the receding tide deposits again the drift-wood in the sand from whence it came. He knows full well that the power is in the tide and not in the wood. Realizing his own nothingness he would say with the Apostle Paul, "By the grace of God I am what I am."

INTRODUCTION

In the shaping of history, from time to time there have appeared on the horizon men of great leadership ability who have stood stedfast for the causes of right in the swell of the rising and ebbing tides of times and movements.

No association of men, bound together by a common task, have done more to elevate human life and the advancement of the Kingdom of God, than those men down through the ages who have been divinely called to be the messengers of the Lord in this world. Their class might be called the guild of itinerant preachers and founders of the schools of the prophets. Be it Elijah the Prophet, Paul the Apostle, the great Origen, John Calvin, Charles Finney; or Jesus who is the greatest of all combined together and the strength of all. They have proclaimed clearly and fearlessly the word of God in the power of the Spirit of God. Through their works God has produced the birth of eternity in the souls of men, the formation of the Church of God, enlightenment of civilizations, the relieving of human suffering from miracles at their hands, the raising of hospitals, the birth of charity and philanthropy in the hearts of men, and the rise of institutions of learning, to name a few of the blessings of God which have come through the efforts of these men.

The autobiographer of our book follows in the train of these followers of Christ. He was an itinerant preacher of the gospel during the first quarter of the twentieth century. In simple, straightforward language he writes of his labors. The young minister Albert F. Gray, being a child of his times, went from one appointment to another, be it town or the countryside, under the direction of the Spirit of God and driven by an overwhelming desire to extend the work of his living Lord, that of spreading the gospel of redemption through the blood of Christ, the indwelling of the Holy Spirit, the edifying of the Church, and the working of miracles. As the autobiographer relates the effects that his ministry had on the people of the frontiers in the West, in the great new country of America, the reader is impressed with the humbleness of this man. He writes of the profound changes which occurred in the lives of those who received his message, yet in a matter-of-fact style as related to his labors. Men and women, who later became influential leaders in the Church, were converted under his preaching, and whole families by the scores and hundreds who even today comprise a sizeable segment of the membership of the Churches of God in the West were initially introduced to the gospel through his ministry.

After a few years in the preaching ministry our autobiographer sensed deeply the need for the forming of an institution for the training of the ministry and the education of the youth of the Church. Working with colleagues in the founding of an institution of higher education of the Church of God in the West, it was he among the other educators who endured the troublesome and erratic turn of events which always accompany the early beginnings of any worthwhile enterprise and became the first president of the college with a continuous history, Pacific Bible College and later named Warner Pacific College.

President of the young college, our autobiographer, gave the leadership necessary to build the foundation needed for an institution of higher learning upon which the superstructure of the college might be built to serve succeeding generations in academic depth, spiritual enrichment of the Christian faith, and the ever broadening demands being placed on institutions of education today.

If in any case it can be said that the excellence of an institution is the length of the shadow of its chief executive, it can be said of the founding president of Warner Pacific College. It is fortunate indeed that this founder is leaving for posterity, particularly alumni, faculty, and friends, a history of the establishment and early days of this college through his autobiography.

For this service in addition to that of his ministry in the Church in general, I recommend *Time and Tides on the Western Shore* by Albert F. Gray, president emeritus of Warner Pacific College.

Louis F. Gough
President
Warner Pacific College
March 7, 1966

ANCESTRY

Like most Americans I am of mixed blood. My ancestors came from northern Europe and consisted of English, Scotch, Irish, and German-Swiss strains. One of my ancestors lived in America at the time of the Revolutionary War but being a Tory migrated to Canada. I doubt that any of my ancestors came over in the Mayflower but I cannot be sure as I had about two thousand ancestors at that time. But I am quite sure that some of my ancestors sailed with Noah in the Ark. Also I am sure that they were a healthy race for none of them died in infancy. However I am content simply to call myself an American.

A British soldier, Howarth by name, fought in the battle of Lundy's Lane in the war of 1812. He happened to live on the Canadian side of the Niagara River; had he lived on the American side likely he would have been an American soldier. He is buried at Fingal, Ontario, where he lived and reared his family. One of his daughters was named Julia.

Jacob Baldwin was born in Switzerland, February 9, 1826. His parents brought him to Ontario at the age of two. When grown he married Julia Howarth. These were the parents of my mother, Mary Baldwin, who was born at Fingal, Ontario, June 13, 1853.

William Gray came from a family of Scotch Highlanders who had moved to northern Ireland where William was born. Here he married an Irish girl. After a time they migrated to Ontario where George Alexander was born at Allanburg, April 9, 1844. When grown George married a lady named Culver. They had a son, Charles Edward. Shortly after the birth of Charles his mother died. Later George married Mary Baldwin, November 12, 1873, at Fingal, Ontario. This was the beginning of the family of which I am the youngest member.

My parents moved to Mt. Bridges, Ontario, where their first

1

child, Nettie Rosella, was born, April 7, 1875. Later they moved father west to Strathroy where William James was born, August 7, 1877.

Not long after this father heard the call of adventure and took his family to the great new West stopping at Pembina, Dakota Territory where John Franklin was born October 3, 1879. Ada Beatrice was born at Drayton, a nearby town, February 5, 1882.

These were days of poverty and hardship. Father would say, "It is no disgrace to be poor but it is mighty inconvenient." The winter at Drayton was very severe with the temperature going as low as sixty below zero with lots of snow.

The family lived in a sod house. One morning it seemed the sun would never come up as the house remained dark all forenoon. It happened the house had been snowed completely over. A neighbor brought his shovel and opened a way to the door.

In those days the government was very generous in giving land to new settlers. Father received a preemption, a timber claim and a homestead. He disposed of the first two to enable him to develop the homestead which consisted of 160 acres of fertile, level soil in the Red River Valley, called the bread-basket of the world. This property is described as the southeast quarter of Section 9, Township 139, Range 52, also called Midland Township, Dakota Territory. This home, six miles from St. Thomas is where George Henry was born April 18, 1884, and I was born March 18, 1886.

EARLY CHILDHOOD

There was a celebration at the White House in Washington on the day I was born. Whether this was a good omen or no I cannot tell. It was an important day for President Grover Cleveland as it was his birthday. But an unheralded event on the plains of Dakota was of greater importance to me as it was the initial day of my entire career. Everything that has happened to me since is traceable to that day. I was named Albert after my mother's favorite uncle, Albert Graves, and Frederick after the son of the midwife who helped welcome me into this world.

A great disappointment of my life is that I do not remember my father as he died when I was twenty months old. All summer of 1887 he felt that would be his last year and told mother so. This was not on account of any illness but was a premonition of some sort. In the fall he took pneumonia and died November 23. Thus my mother was left a widow at the age of 34 with six children of her own and a stepson. Although she had offers of marriage she spurned them all remaining true to the memory of the one man whom she considered perfect. She remained a widow for 47 years.

We remained on the farm for two years after father's death then rented the place and moved to be with Grandfather Baldwin at his home near Walshville on the Red River. My earliest remembrance concerns the night before we left our home. I looked out the door into the darkness of the night. I do not remember much that I saw but the feeling of fear and wonder stayed with me. The next day we traveled to Grandfather's home where we were to remain for the next two years.

I recall a number of happenings at Grandfather's home. One day we boys were running around the barn. I was carrying a pitchfork and in my hurry I ran it through my foot. The tine did not strike a bone so none were broken. My foot healed but I still have the scar.

One day we found a hen's nest with many eggs in it. We did not know whether they were fresh or not. Somehow Frank had learned that a good egg will sink in water while a bad one will float. He took the eggs in his hat to the brink of the river and began to throw them in to see if they were good or not. This seemed like a waste of good eggs but I thought anything Frank would do must be right. Frank had a brass handled knife which he carried in his hand much of the time. When the eggs were gone the knife had disappeared too. Apparently it did not float.

The day I was five years of age a man named Dawes came to

3

see mother and, as one courting a widow should do, he brought candy for the children. I thought that since it was my birthday I should have all the candy. I demanded George's piece so mother sent him to the barn to escape my avarice.

One day Will was working under a tree making a bow and arrow. He tried to split a board with a doublebitted axe. The axe struck a limb and bounced back cutting his scalp. He was not hurt much but the accident could have been fatal.

It became necessary for mother to return to St. Thomas occasionally to look after the farm. One time while she was gone I became sick with chickenpox. Grandfather did not put me to bed but fed me liquid tar. This was his remedy for everything. I was glad when mother returned to look after me. She did not leave me behind after that but the next time took me with her.

Grandfather lived in a log house so every fall he would replaster the cracks between the logs with barnyard plaster mixed with lime. This was quite effective in keeping out the wind.

Bridges across the Red River were few and far between. There were occasional ferries for crossing the river. Grandfather operated one. In those days steamboats ran from Grand Forks to Winnepeg. As a boat would approach Grandfather's ferry the boat would whistle that he might come and lower his ferry rope. One day a visitor stopped for a meal. He was a ventriquilist. During the meal he whistled like a steam boat. Grandfather sprang from the table and ran to his ferry to lower the rope, but no boat appeared. He was not very happy over this prank.

It was October 3, 1891, when we loaded our belongings onto a hayrack and moved to Grand Forks. It took us all day to drive the 25 miles. We moved into a house belonging to Uncle Will Baldwin located at 614 9th Avenue (now 5th Ave., S.). The house was not warmly built and the winter was very cold. Here we lived for three years. The wheat crops were quite good so mother bought a lot and built a house. It was 1½ stories 14' x 24' with 5 rooms and cost $400.00. We moved in October 3, 1894 which was Frank's birthday.

4

Upon arriving in Grand Forks we spent a few days with Uncle John Baldwin. He conducted a dray business and Will worked for him. There was a swing at the barn where Will would swing and we small boys would run across behind the swing. I made it across but as I started back the swing board struck my head cutting my scalp and throwing me into a pile of bricks. This raised a ridge on each side of my skull so that my head is about balanced. Mother was away at church so Uncle Robert Fletcher fixed my wound with courtplaster.

In the spring of 1894 there came to Grand Forks a terrible epidemic of typhoid fever in which more than 300 people died. My brother Frank was one of them. He was fourteen years old. Before he became sick he had been baptized and was a good Christian boy. His death was a severe shock to all of us. Will, who was then sixteen, joined the Baptist church and was baptized. Not long after he attended a revival held by a Free Methodist minister in which he was soundly converted. Soon after this he joined the Salvation Army where he became a diligent soldier. For a few months he traveled in a brass band for the Army in several northern states. He was commissioned a Lieutenant.

After coming to Washington Will came in fully with the Church of God and served as an active member in Spokane and later in Seattle. For years he served as trustee and treasurer and, though not a minister, he served on campmeeting boards. He gave very liberally in establishing Pacific Bible College.

My brother George entered the ministry at about the same time as I did. His early ministry was spent in Western Canada where he served as an evangelist. Upon returning to Spokane he became pastor of the Hillyard church and later of the Dean Avenue church. Later he pastored the church in Grants Pass for several years. After leaving Grants Pass he established a rural church near Cave Junction, which was moved to town. He pastored this church seventeen years till he was forced to resign on account of failing health.

My sister Ada, even in her tender age, was deeply interested in spiritual things and had she lived doubtless she would have become an effective church worker.

I do appreciate very much the encouragement I received from my family.

EARLY SCHOOL DAYS

I became six years of age on Friday and started to school the following Monday. George had entered school the previous September and was in the first grade. Mother wanted me in the same class with George. The teacher tested me before the chart and found how little I knew so put me in the chart (C) class. The following September I entered grade one, A class.

There is little to remember from my first grade. For one thing we celebrated Columbus day by making paper Spanish flags just 400 years after the discovery of America. This year also vocal music was introduced in the public schools in all grades.

It was in the second grade that we celebrated arbor day by planting trees, one for each grade. At the roots of each tree was placed a glass jar containing the names of the members of that grade. My name should be in a jar beneath a tree at Belmont School if the jar has not been destroyed.

It was in the second grade that I reached my lowest depth in deportment. The teacher was questioning a girl and became quite provoked at the girl's ignorance. The girl gave a very dumb answer and I laughed. The teacher was already out of patience so she called me up front and slapped my face for laughing. Since then I have tried not to be too smart. I guess this incident helped me as thereafter I always received high grades in deportment.

I remember nothing of importance that happened while I was in the third grade. But it was about this time that there was a smallpox scare and all children were to be vaccinated. Mother felt that she could not afford to have all of us vaccinated separately so our doctor Fawsett vaccinated Nettie, then when her arm became sore he vaccinated the rest of us from her scab. When he vaccinated me he seid, "hereafter you will always be part girl."

6

I was nine years old when I finished the third grade. Mother took me to Dr. Fawsett for an examination. He had me lie on a couch and put a Bible under my head and said, "This is the best pillow you will ever have under your head." It seemed very hard to me but later I understood what he meant.

The doctor's examination showed my heart to be twice its normal size and my pulse very slow. He said he could do nothing for me but that as I was young I might outgrow my condition. He advised that I be kept out of school for a year, and I was. But before the year was up Brother G. W. Bailey held a tent meeting to which mother took me to receive prayer for healing. Brother Bailey prayed for me and though my pulse remains slow my heart has given me very little trouble and seems quite normal.

The following September I returned to school in the fourth grade. Our teacher was a good Christian lady who opened each day with the Lord's Prayer. It was in this grade that I had my only experience of being tardy. George and I had moved wood into the woodshed in the noon hour and it took longer than we had realized. Just as we entered the school door the tardy bell rang. George's teacher did not count him tardy as he was inside the building but mine marked me tardy as I was not yet in our room.

In the fifth grade I had a good Christian teacher. We got along well till March 4, 1898. That day she said, "There is a boy in the A class who has not studied but has played with his pencil all afternoon: I am taking 5% from his grade in deportment." I knew she meant me, but she did not know I was sick. That night I went to bed with typhoid fever and before I was well again the school year was over, and the Spannsh-American war was about over.

A few days after I became sick Will came down with the fever also. Both of us were very sick at the same time. This was almost more than mother could bear. It was four years since the epidemic of typhoid fever in which my brother Frank died. Ada came down with the same disease shortly after and did not fully

7

recover but died three years later. Will mother now lose two more of her family?

We had a good doctor who did all he could for us. Will recovered before I did. At times I was very low and the doctor despaired of my life. Uncle Will Baldwin prayed for me and I began to improve and eventually became entirely well with no apparent remaining effects of the disease.

Many years after I learned that when I was very low one day mother said to the family concerning me, "He is going to get well and he is going to preach the gospel." How she knew this I cannot tell. It may be she dedicated me to the Lord and he gave her this assurance. She believed in such communications for father had told her of his forthcoming death and a few months before his death Frank told her he would not live a year, and he did not.

When September came again I returned to school expecting to take the fifth grade over as I had lost the last three months. But my teacher appealed to the superintendent to permit me to go to the sixth grade on condition. After examining my grades he agreed to let me do so. I found the first few weeks quite difficult but soon I caught up and found myself with the four or five best students of the class. Perhaps I could have been the star had I tried but I was glad for others to do as well or better than I if they could.

The seventh and eight grades were taken with little that was unusual. We had the "three R's" with other important subjects. Art and music were included. I did not do well in art but was better in music and mathematics. Music was taught in all grades and in the seventh and eighth grades we sang on sight rather difficult music such as selections from "Elijah." In math I worked problems that none of my classmates could get and one problem that a teacher said could not be solved.

Early in 1901 mother and Will filed on homesteads in Bottineau County and moved there leaving me in Grand Forks to finish the eighth grade. My teacher arranged for me to take my final test early so I could go to the farm. On June 1 I took my final test which ended my formal secular education.

George had written me to come to Bottineau Wednesday but I failed to receive his letter. I went on Monday and found no one in town to meet me. I found a neighbor, Mr. Kelly, who took me as far as his place then I walked the last seven miles. Our place was 22 miles from Bottineau, our nearest town.

As the country was newly settled there were few if any children for many miles which left no opportunity for me to go on to High School.

In the fall of 1902, mother, Nettie and I went to Spokane. Shortly after our arrival I applied to enter High School but as the term was half over I was not accepted. I was advised to take the eighth grade over but this did not appeal to me.

In early spring Will, George and Alfred (Nettie's husband) came and soon we bought a farm near Cheney where we moved. I was then seventeen.

EARLY BUSINESS VENTURES

After we moved to Grand Forks we kept two cows. We sold one to meet the expenses of Frank's sickness and burial. It was my duty to collect from the neighbors potato peelings, cabbage leaves, etc., for our cows. After we sold our other cow I continued to collect for a neighbor called Gunderson. For this service I received 5c per week. Also Mrs. Rude would give me hot cookies most every day for taking her peelings away, so I worked both ends. One Saturday Mrs. Gunderson said she had no nickel for me so I quit right then.

I got a job delivering a paper called The Daily Record which went to a number of business firms for which I received $1.00 per month. My boss quit business owing me $1.50. I called several times to collect but he always put me off. I kept on coming till one day some business men were visiting him. I think he was ashamed to refuse me in their presence so he paid me in full.

On Saturdays I would ride with a grocery delivery man and

help him deliver groceries for which he paid me 25c each Saturday.

Three summers, 1898 to 1900, I spent part of my vacation on Thomas H. Johnston's farm, 14 miles SW of Grand Forks. I received no pay but I earned my board and learned something about farming which was helpful to me later at our Bottineau home.

At Bottineau I shocked ten acres of wheat for a neighbor for which he paid me $5.00. Also I worked for Bush and Shetler on their threshing machine cutting bands for $2.00 a day.

Later on I worked some on a farm and also did some clerking. But I had no plans either to become a farmer or a business man. God had other plans for me.

EARLY RELIGIOUS LIFE

My parents were married in the Baptist Church at Fingal, Ontario. After moving to Dakota they became members of the Baptist Church at St. Thomas, our home town. My father was a deacon in this church at the time of his death.

Upon moving to Grand Forks we attended the Baptist Church. I attended this Sunday School for seven or eight years. The superintendent was R. B. Griffith, who was one of the chief merchants of the state. After he had served as superintendent for several years the children were asked to bring money with which to buy him a chair. Mother was disgusted that the children should be asked to buy a chair for this rich man so she said to me, "I don't care if you never go to that Sunday School again," so I quit going.

Mother spoke hastily on this occasion but this was not her usual way of speaking. She did not talk about religion to us very much but her regular family worship was a strong influence on the whole family.

My first experience with a guilty conscience occurred when I was gathering potato peelings. I saw a small wooden shelf in what appeared to be a pile of trash at the rear of Mr. Cadwell's house. I looked at it and wanted it, but I felt I had no right to take it. But after some hesitation I took it. But I found no joy in possessing it for my conscience troubled me. I showed it to mother and told her I had found it but did not say where. She saw it had no value so asked no questions. She did not know how troubled I was. I went from her presence feeling worse for I had not told her the whole truth. I was deeply troubled.

A few days later Archie Elvrum, who lived next to Cadwells, saw the shelf and claimed it as his. I was glad for him to take it as I wanted it off of my hands.

At another time, when on my way to Sunday School with two older boys, we decided not to put our pennies in the collection but to spend them for candy on the way home so we stopped at Tripanier's drug store to spend our money. Here we found a small pinball machine. We each bought a ball to drop in the machine. The other boys knew how to operate it so as not to lose. They told me how to hold the ball but I didn't try so my ball landed on "O" so I lost. I was really glad that I did lose for I knew I was doing wrong. I never gambled again. I would play marbles with the boys but I always refused to play for keeps.

Late in 1894 the Salvation Army came to Grand Forks. One of their first converts was a neighbor of ours who was a bad drunkard. We became quite interested in the Army; Will joined, and Ada would have joined but was too young, but she became what they called a Junior Soldier.

Junior meetings were held on Saturday afternoons. One Friday Ada said to me, "Tomorrow we are going to the Junior meeting and you must get saved." So I went to the mourner's bench and was really saved. George was saved a week later. While I prayed I seemed to feel the Lord cleaning out my heart. There ran through my mind the words of the song:

'Twas a happy day, and no mistake
When Jesus from my heart did take
That load of sin that made it ache
And filled my soul with joy.

11

This experience had a great effect on all my future.

Interest in the Army ran high. The boys and girls of the city were not the last to become enthusiastic about it. Some of the children of our neighborhood started a Salvation Army of their own. They obtained S's and red braid and the girls turned down the brims of their hats to make them look like poke bonnets and the boys who could got red sweaters. They marched the streets with flags waving and beating tin pans for drums and tambourines.

But alas! This miniature Army came to a tragic end. When the officers of the real Salvation Army learned of it they told these young folks that they were without authority thus to imitate the Salvation Army. The project stopped as suddenly as it had started. But young people cannot be stopped from questioning: they wished to know who gave General Booth authority to start his Army.

Soon after this Ada organized a little religious society of her own. But she was wiser than these other young folks as she did not copy the Army. She called hers the Junior Band. We did not wear Salvation Army badges but our badge was a little white bow. One day my school teacher asked me if I belonged to the W.C.T.U. We did not realize we were infringing on that organization.

At this time Uncle Will Baldwin's house, near ours, was vacant so we got permission to hold meetings in it. We fixed a platform and seats and invited the neighbor children in. We sang and played our instruments, such as they were, and held meeting. We tried to get the children to the penitent form and I doubt not that some of them were really saved.

But when Mrs. Elvrum learned of it she told us it was very wicked to play religion and have mock meetings so we quit. But I think we were as sincere as many of the older people were.

It was in November, 1895, that G. W. Bailey and J. C. Peterman, ministers of the church of God, came to Grand Forks. A group of people interested in holiness were holding cottage meetings. This group included Methodists, Baptists, Salvationists, Free Methodists and a few others. This group held a meeting at our home which was attended by Brother Bailey. After several had bragged about their churches Brother Bailey gave them a strong speech against division based on I Cor. 1 and 3. I sat on the stairs and listened. Mother and Uncle Will Baldwin were soon won to the truth. A congregation of the Church of God in Grand Forks was begun at that time. Soon mother would go about the house singing:

"Oh glory to Jesus we hail the bright day
And high on our banners salvation display,
The mists of confusion are passing away."

Some of those present at that meeting resented the message and rejected the truth, including their leader, Joe Nixon, a Free Methodist minister. I liked Nixon so was somewhat prejudiced against the new preachers. For a little while I was Baptist, Salvationist and saint but eventually was won over to the truth.

The church in Grand Forks made good progress, soon campmeetings were held there. Ministers attending early campmeetings included C. H. and Mary Tubbs, J. C. Peterman and Wm. G. Schell. In 1899 Thomas Nelson and D. O. Teasley were present.

At the close of the 1899 meeting D. O. Teasley took the grip (flu) and mother took him to our home to care for him. I got to know him and to like him very much. He was a good preacher and song writer and developed into a very versatile man becoming a strong leader among us. His influence on me was very helpful in making me what I have become.

For a few years after my conversion I had my ups and downs. I did not attend church regularly. A few months after we were saved George and I were playing with other boys at the corner of 8th Ave. (now 4th S) and Cottonwood Street. The lamp lighter drove up in his cart to light the street lamp and visited a while. He offered some of the boys his pipe and a few of them smoked. George stood looking on, then stepped forward and took a few puffs. I knew he had given up but I held on a while longer.

One Saturday morning, while playing with Bun Bird in his back yard, some boys twitted me about being a Salvationist. Bun came to my rescue by saying, "Aw, go on, he aint no Salvation." I said nothing; then I felt I had denied my Savior. I had given up and felt that the battle was over, somewhat like a soldier who has been taken a prisoner of war.

Some time later a revival was being held in the Methodist church and I knew I would be urged to attend. But I did not want to go for I was strongly prejudiced against all sectism. I had not been getting along well spiritually so before going to the meeting I went to my room and prayed, "Lord forgive me and save me for Jesus' sake, Amen." I am afraid my repentance was not very sincere but anyway I headed off those who would have tried to drag me to a sectarian altar.

One day the Baptist minister visited our house and as I was going to town he walked along with me. On the way he told me that Henry Sather, a friend of mine, would be baptized soon and asked if I would like to be baptized at the same time. I hedged a bit so he said, "Perhaps you would like to discuss the matter with your mother first." He did not even ask me if I was saved.

Although I did not keep the victory all the time during my early teens I was able, through God's goodness to lead a clean life, better than many professed Christians. I can testify that God saved me from many sins for it is as great a victory to be kept from entering sin as it is to be pulled out of sin. At no time have profane words or vile language passed my lips. I wish I could say as much for my ears but one does not always choose what he hears. I have never smoked tobacco but a few times I smoked dried corn silk. I guess it is not habit forming for I did not get the habit. On two occasions, in later life, I tasted liquor. One time I ordered a soft drink and was served wine. It tasted very repugnant. The other occasion was at a church service of communion where fermented wine was used, though watered down.

One time two of us boys saw a man, whom we knew, take a

14

chew of tobacco. As a prank we asked him to give us a chew. He handed us his plug. The other boy took a big bite which made him so sick he had to go to bed. I took a little nibble but as I did not like it I spit it out. The only other time I tasted tobacco was when I greeted a brother (?) with a holy kiss: he had a chew of tobacco in his mouth. I tell these things not to boast of myself but to thank God for keeping me from going far into sin.

While we lived in Bottineau County in the long winter nights mother would read to us from "The Secret of Salvation," by E. E. Byrum. I was impressed so on January 2, 1902, I went to the barn and renewed my covenant with the Lord. Since that time I have not consciously and deliberately sinned against God. I have made mistakes and failures but I thank him for keeping me from wilful sin. I have found that his grace is sufficient.

MY SANCTIFICATION

While attending the Salvation Army Junior meetings our leader told us one day that we should watch our feelings when tempted. She said sometime we might feel like saying, "If I was not a Christian I would fight you." This came close to me for I had felt that very way at times. I wished she would tell us what to do about it but she did not.

I was not inclined to look for trouble but I was unable to control my temper. I would fly mad easily, then soon get over it. One time our cow got frightened and upset me and spilled the milk. I beat her with the milk stool, then put my arm around her neck and begged her pardon.

While we were living in Bottineau County the railroad was extended and a new town named Souris sprang up at the end of the line which was about six miles from our home. Will opened a store in the new town and George worked for him. Mother had gone to Grand Forks to attend the campmeeting so I was home alone through the days. I did some reading and one book I read was entitled Perfect Love. While reading this book I received a great blessing. I felt so happy I wanted to tell it but our nearest neighbor lived a mile away and there were no telephones. So I went outdoors and put my arm around the calf's neck while I sang with all my heart. I wrote mother that I had received perfect love. But alas, I soon found that I was without power to control my temper but that it controlled me. Also other defects remained.

In the fall mother and I returned to Grand Forks to prepare to move to Spokane. While there we attended the church of God on Cottonwood Street on Sunday morning. We heard Brother Nels Renbeck preach though I do not remember what he said. I went to the altar to seek sanctification. Brother Thomas Nelson came to help me. After a few remarks he asked me, "Are you all on the altar?" I replied, "I believe I am." He said, "The Bible says the altar sanctifies the gift. If you are on the altar who is sanctified?" I replied, "I must be." He replied, "Amen; take it by faith and go on your way." But again I experienced no change.

After we reached Spokane I heard Brother Jake Peterman preach a very searching sermon which convinced me I did not have the experience. I resolved this time to seek it by myself. I went to my room and got on my knees and prayed like this, "Lord, you have said you are more willing to give the Holy Ghost to your sons who ask than a father is to give good gifts to his children. I am asking you to give me the Holy Ghost and to sanctify me wholly. I believe you do it. Amen." But again nothing happened.

Mother, George and I attended the Assembly Meeting at the Saints' Home near Colfax in November, 1903. There were a number of ministers present including A. D. Khan of India. After other soul-searching sermons Sister Amanda Brown preached one afternoon. I do not remember what she said but between her sermon and the night meeting I spent the time in prayer. The Lord began to talk to me and to tell me what I must do. To one thing after another I said, "Yes Lord, I will," Finally he said, "I want you to preach the gospel." I replied, "Why, Lord, I cannot do that, I can scarcely get up enough courage to testify in the presence of these ministers, I cannot preach." The Lord said, "I do not ask you to preach just yet, but after while." Still I plead, "Lord, I am not able." To which he replied, "I know you are not able yet, but I will make you able." I surrendered, "Lord, if you will make me able I will." This completed my consecration.

That night I went to the altar to receive sanctification. Brothers S. H. Eddings, W. J. Baldwin and William Ebel came to help me. They asked me a number of questions but these were not needed as all problems were settled between me and the Lord in the afternoon. Then they laid their hands on my head and prayed God to sanctify me and fill me with the Holy Ghost. While they were praying I felt something like an electric shock go from their hands to my heart. Then there was diffused throughout my entire body a glow of warmth. This continued for half an hour. I did not jump, shout or talk in tongues; in fact I did not speak. There was a feeling of "blessed quietness," so clean, so pure, so holy. I knew God had touched me and the Holy Ghost had sanctified me.

Although this was a great miracle that I can never forget, it does not tell the full story. From that time on I was a new man. I have suffered opposition and persecution while I remained calm and unruffled. I have been cursed and have had rocks and eggs thrown at me, and even been threatened with death and through it all I kept serene peace in my soul. Even "righteous indignation" could not arouse my temper beyond control. Although naturally timid I have not feared to preach to large audiences. I have not aspired to be a great preacher, for I know my own weakness, but I trusted God "to make me able." I am not bothered with stage fright for I have no reputation to defend. I am aware that only "by the grace of God I am what I am."

Through the baptism of the Holy Ghost I received certain gifts through which God has helped me to serve. I have not tried to display these but leave them for others to discover. Except as God works through me I am useless.

Two days after I was sanctified I was baptized in Union

Creek which flows through the camp ground. My brother George, Clinton Chapman, and perhaps Harry Cooper were baptized also. As I entered the water I felt I was leaving the whole world behind. It was like a spiritual funeral. We all came out of the watery grave with hands held high in victory. Four of us became ministers.

Following the baptism was an ordinance in which, for the first time, I partook of the Lord's supper and foot washing. Brother Eddings, who baptized us, was ordained a minister at that service.

Shortly after my sanctification I went with Will to see a house in which he was interested. The basement was vacant except for a battery on a shelf. I thought I would like to have it but knew I had no right to it and had no thought of taking it. But the devil said, "You coveted that battery: sanctified people don't covet." But as I had no evil intention I soon defeated him.

About that time George slapped me on the back in play; a shiver went up my spine. The devil said, "sanctified people don't feel that way." But I soon defeated the devil for I had no feeling of anger or resentment. I knew the feeling was physical.

The devil soon gave up trying to cause me to doubt my experience of sanctification for he knew that I knew that he knew my experience was genuine. Never once have I regretted the consecratation I made. I do not regret entering the ministry and never once have I wished to leave it. I am well aware of my limitations and frailty but I have remained true to my covenant wth the Lord. Through God's grace I have been kept free from wilful and conscious disobedience. Since the day I was sanctified and baptized with the Holy Spirit I have been able to keep the victory. To God be the glory.

ENTERING THE MINISTRY

At the time of my sanctification I was definitely called to the ministry but now the big question was how to get started. I did not tell anyone about my call for it seemed too sacred to talk about. I just waited on the Lord to bring it about.

One day I heard my uncle, W. J. Baldwin, speak about plans to hold a meeting at Cheney. At once I felt a desire to go with him; so I prayed, "Lord, if you want me to go with him have him ask me." Soon he told me about the meeting and asked me to pray about going with him. I did not need to pray further about it but did not tell him right away. Later I hold him I would go. I celebrated my eighteenth birthday while on my first trip in gospel work.

Shortly after this Uncle Will asked me to go with him on a trip north. After prayer I felt led to do so. We went to see a certain brother named Joe Blossom who lived near Camdon on the side of Mount Baldy (now Mount Spokane). This brother had been active in church in Spokane but had become isolated. Our mission was somewhat like that of Barnabas when he went to Tarsus to seek Paul but ours was not so successful. We went by train, about 30 miles from Spokane, then walked back, arriving at a little town about dark where we stopped over night in a hotel (50c for the two of us) and walked on to Hillyard the next day where we took a street car the rest of the way into Spokane.

Shortly after this we made a trip by bicycle to Chester where we visited a Negro family, then on to Moran Prairie where we visited a woman suffering from rheumatism. When Uncle Will prayed she was instantly healed and her joints came loose. From there we went to Rockford and Fairfield visiting the brethren, mostly Germans.

Our next trip was to Creston, Washington, where there was a very spiritual congregation pastored by Brother V. C. Maiden, who later became a missionary to India. From there we went to Peach, now covered by backwater from Grand Coulee Dam, where we visited Brother Fred Timm. It was on April 18 that I had my first glimpse of the Columbia River.

Uncle Will went east to attend the campmeeting at Moundsville, W. Va. This left me free for the summer. I spent the time studying and attending campmeetings. I attended the Daisy campmeeting north of Spokane about 80 miles. This was a meeting where people really camped. Each family had its own stove and table. Single persons, like myself, were invited out to eat. I never knew where I would eat my next meal but was always invited by somebody. There was no charge for this hospitality but one was expected to give what he could toward the expense of the meeting.

After the Daisy meeting I attended the Creston campmeeting. Among the preachers present were Willis M. Brown and his son Charley. Willis was widely known for his healing ministry. He was also a powerful preacher. Charley, years later, became editor of the Gospel Trumpet.

Following this campmeeting one was held in Spokane. Charley was present at this meeting also. I still remember one of his sermons. He was 20 years old at that time and unmarried. Sister Nettie (Fields) Berghouse would take Charley's sermons down in shorthand. This bothered him so she would go outside the tent where she could hear but he could not see her. A young man who attended the meeting told me his name was Frank Goss, Evangelist. He said no one could remember his name. I guess that mixed it in my mind for I have had no difficulty recalling it since.

During the fall and winter of 1903-04 the church in Spokane held services in a hall on South Sherman Street. There was no regular pastor but Sister Rose Graham was looked to as leader. Frequently such ministers as J. C. Peterman and O. A. and Ida M. Chapman would drop in and preach. The following spring a hall was rented on Mallon Avenue near Monroe Street. One Sunday morning as I was on my way to Sunday School I felt impressed that I should teach the adult class that morning. There were two classes, one for adults and one for children. I said, "Lord, if you want me to teach this class have Sister Graham or Brother Forsyth ask me to do so." As it happened each of them asked me, so I did so, and fairly well considering it was my first attempt at teaching.

About the same time the church became interested in buying

a property and building a church. A committee located a property at the corner of Olive (now Trent) and Superior Streets and bordering on Spokane River. It was decided to buy and build.

Brother Peterman preached to us and called for pledges for this purpose. He told how to decide how much to pledge. He had us all kneel down and ask God how much to pledge. He said the first amount that came to one's mind would be from the Lord. He said if the devil says that is too much double it and he will flee. I pledged $100.00 to be paid in two years. I didn't know where it would come from as that was more money than I had owned in my whole life, but it was paid before the year was up. One young lady pledged $400.00 though her income was $2.50 per week plus board and room. She was unable to pay her pledge and it was forgiven.

But enough money was raised and the Missionary Home was built at a cost of $4,000.00 plus much donated labor. I worked many days on the building without pay, besides my cash pledge.

Again the time had come to attend the Assembly Meeting at the Saints' Home. A year had passed since I had been gloriously sanctified. This had been a happy year in which I had made much spiritual progress. This meeting was attended by F. G. Smith and his wife as well as several local ministers. I still remember some of Brother Smith's sermons.

Leaving the Saints' Home I went with Brothers Peterman and Baldwin and Charles Walker to Kippen, Idaho, where we held a meeting at Ford's Mill. We passed through Lewiston, Idaho, where we stayed over night and where we met a Brother Slaughter, a plasterer. The next day we drove on to Kippen. A good meeting was held there.

Brother Peterman had been invited to Eltopia, a small town near Pasco. He and Brother Baldwin planned to go there after the Kippen meeting should close and they invited me to go along. As always I prayed about it. I went to the woods to pray after dark. I am sure no one could see me or hear me pray. I asked the Lord whether he would have me go with them. I heard a voice cry loudly "Yes." It startled me as I was sure no one knew I was there. I saw a lantern hanging at the barn some distance away. I wondered if the voice came from there. I watched and listened for a while but I saw no one and heard not another sound. I wondered whether God really spoke to me. Anyway I accepted the answer and went with them.

When we arrived at Eltopia we found Brother G. W. Alexander already there. We remained and helped him a few days then went on to Yakima. Brother Alexander later became a missionary to Japan. The meeting at Yakima continued through Christmas day. It was held in the little church on West B street. It was quite helpful to the church where there had been some division. I started for my home at Spokane Christmas night.

A few days after Christmas Brother Baldwin went to Stites, Idaho, to hold a meeting. He had asked me to go with him, but as I had been away from home on Christmas I desired to remain home for New Years. I thought the Lord would be willing for that, so I waited till January 2, 1905, when I went by train from Spokane to Stites, a distance of about 200 miles. It took all day to make the trip so I arrived at dark.

As no one knew I was coming there was no one at the train to meet me, so I followed the crowd and soon found myself in the Post Office where the people waited for the mail to be distributed. While the people were waiting I heard them talk about the meeting. When the others had received their mail, and Brother Baldwin had not come, I asked for my mail, though I knew I would receive none. Then I asked if there was mail for W. J. Baldwin. The postmaster replied that he had ordered his mail forwarded to Moscow. This left me in confusion.

I thought there must be a mistake for people were talking about the meeting, and as it was about meeting time and people were heading toward the meeting house I followed the crowd. Sure enough there was a meeting but it was being held by a Baptist minister. Realizing the town was too small for two meetings at once Brother Baldwin had returned to Moscow, about half way back to Spokane. What was I to do now, 200 miles from home with 60 cents in my pocket.

The minister preached on "Angels and Hornets." He said it was one of his poorest sermons which he saved for Monday nights. At the close of the service I stood around for a while hoping some person might notice that I was a stranger and offer me lodging. No one spoke to me or looked at me. I stepped out into the night.

It was mid-winter though not so very cold. The ground was covered with a thin coat of snow which lessened the darkness and made it not difficult for me to see my way as I started on my return trip. On and on I walked down the railroad track carrying my grip. I passed through Kooskia and on to Kamiah. By this time I had walked ten miles and had become tired and sleepy. I came to a grain warehouse with the door partly open so I entered and lay down with my grip for a pillow. I slept a short while then awoke cold so walked on.

Brother A. J. Stuart, who later was a very active minister in Montana, was at that time a grain dealer in Kamiah. He says it was his warehouse where I slept that night.

Quite early in the morning I reached Greer where I stopped at a store and spent ten cents for crackers which I ate as I walked on. I had not eaten a meal since I left Spokane.

On and on I trudged down the railroad track. The ties were not spaced properly for convenient walking so I stubbed my toes with the result that I lost one of my toenails.

I had learned that there was a family of saints living at Orofino. I kept trying to remember their name but could not quite think of it. But when I reached town I asked a man on the street where Alleneters lived. He knew who I meant and told me to go on to the end of the sidewalk and there I would find them. I supposed that would be a short way but the walk turned up Orofine Creek which I followed for two miles more before reaching the home of George Alteneder who was an old-time saint, a convert of Barney E. Warren and S. L. Speck. I was met at the door by his daughter who recognized me having seen me at the Saints Home Assembly a few weeks before. I was invited in and made welcome.

Brother Alteneder and his family treated me well and kept me over night. The next morning, after breakfast, I thanked them for their hospitality and said I would be going on. He asked where I was going, and when I said that I was going to Moscow he said, "The train has already gone." I replied, "I am not going by train." He then asked if I had no money and when I admitted it he said he would not allow one of God's servants to walk out of town but that I should stay till tomorrow and he would give me train fare to Moscow. I was glad for this for I was still tired and sore from my 35 miles walk from Stites.

The next morning I took the train for Moscow. I had not been there before and did not know where to find Brother Baldwin. So I followed the same method I had used at Stites and went to the Post Office thinking I might meet Brother Baldwin there. I did not see him but I saw a young man whom I had met also at the Assembly. I asked him if he knew the whereabouts of Brother Baldwin. He said that as soon as he got his mail he would take me to him for he was at their home. This was the home of W. S. Ross, on North Main Street. Here I found Brother Baldwin and thus ended one chapter of my early gospel work.

Before leaving Stites Brother Baldwin wrote me not to come there but to come to Moscow instead, but I had already left before the letter came. My folks read the letter and were much disturbed for they knew I had no money and I had never been so far from home alone before. But I felt no worry. I was somewhat confused but felt no regrets and blamed no one, not even myself. I felt sure the Lord had his hand in it all and that he would work all out to his glory. It was my privilege to return to Stites years later and to reap a good harvest for the Lord.

At the home of Brother Ross I found Brother Baldwin and Brother Joe Conover holding a meeting. The room was small but a few people were in attendance in addition to the Ross family.

In those days no plans were made in advance as to who should preach. When the time came whoever felt he had the message stood to preach. Sometimes it was Brother Baldwin and sometimes it was Brother Conover.

It was on January 13th I felt I had a message. Neither Brother Baldwin nor Brother Conover felt he had the message so they were not surprised when I arose to speak. I spoke on Christian Conduct, reading several scriptures that bore on the subject. This was my first attempt at preaching. Homiletically it was not much of a sermon but God seemed to use it. When I had finished Brother Baldwin, who had worked at threshing grain, arose and said, "We have threshed a few settings of grain in this meeting, tonight we ran the grain through the fanning mill." As the meeting continued a few people were saved including the wife of a county official.

It was planned to close the meeting on Sunday. Brother Conover wished to be at his home at Colfax and Brother Baldwin wished to be at Palouse so they left me to preach at both Sunday services. At the morning service a Methodist lady, Mrs. Ella Collins, was with us. She was greatly moved upon by the Spirit, though perhaps not because of anything I said. That summer she came to the Saints Home campmeeting and was gloriously saved. She became a pillar in the church at Moscow.

Shortly after this I returned to Spokane where I spoke in a prayermeeting. Brother Huffman, a German brother, said to me, "When it comes from de heart it goes to de heart." This was a splendid thought which I have remembered.

After a brief stay in Spokane I returned with Brother Baldwin to Idaho where we visited several small congregations and isolated saints. We stopped at Moscow, Winchester, Woodside, Forest, Kippen, and perhaps a few other places. We held some meetings and visited isolated saints giving them encouragement and our prayers. At a few of these places I preached and gradually took a larger place in the work of the ministry.

On April 7th, 1905, Brother Baldwin and Orpha George were

married at Spokane, I served as best man and Orpha's sister May George was bridesmaid. Shortly after the wedding the four of us went to Creston, Washington, where there was a fine congregation. After the Sunday morning service Brother Guering, who lived some distance from town, invited me home with them for dinner: I accepted. Sister Almira Davis, who was a leader in the church, invited and rather urged me to come to her house, but I kept my promise to go with the Guerings. When it came time to go Brother Guering placed me in the back seat of his hack and May George with me while he and his wife occupied the front seat. I did not know May was going along. This was a violation of proper decorum as boys and girls were not to ride together. Now I understood why Sister Davis was so urgent; she must have known what was up. But it was not my fault for I did not know the plan till too late. May later admitted that she had some interest in me as her second choice but I had no interest in her.

From Creston we went to Peach (now inundated) and held a few services in the school house. Here we met opposition in attempts to harass and annoy the preacher. One night when the stove got warm the whole room smelled of limburger cheese. Not much was accomplished at this place.

We were invited to anther community called Egypt where we held services in the school house. We were well received at this place. Brother and Sister Baldwin both preached and they did most of the preaching. One night, though it was against the rule, they discussed between themselves which should preach but neither felt the message. They concluded the Lord would have me. I knew nothing of this but I felt God had given me a message so when the time came to preach I arose and preached with liberty.

The summer campmeetings were about due. The main meeting is held near Colfax with smaller meetings at other places. I attended four campmeetings that summer. The first was at Daisy. There were a few cases of demon possession at that meeting. Mention of these will be made elsewhere.

Before this meeting Brother J. C. Peterman, who would be one of the principal ministers, spent some days in the woods in prayer and Bible study and came to the meeting well prepared with spiritual power. When I saw how God had blessed him I went to the woods and prayed, "Lord, I must have a great outpouring like you gave Brother Peterman." But it didn't come. The Lord did not intend to use me as he was using Brother Peterman or he would have blessed me too.

In this meeting the enthusiasm of a few people went wild. In a testimony meeting one brother shouted, "Shoot against Babylon: spare no arrows." This led to several harsh statements the climax of which was, "Sectism is just a greased plank for people to slide into hell on."

The next meeting I attended was at Creston. Brother W. J. Henry was present. The first sermon he preached met resistance. He turned to the ministers and asked, "What is the matter here? This is like preaching against a stone wall." But soon he found his target and said, "I'm not going to shoot in another direction."

Following this campmeeting at Creston I attended the larger campmeeting at the Saints Home, as it was formerly called, near Colfax. This was the first of twenty-one consecutive campmeetings I attended at this place. I have returned a few times since.

At this meeting there were a few of us young men who left called to the ministry. One of the ministers preached a strong sermon against the "preach spirit." A special meeting was called to which all of us were summoned. I went at once to see Brother O. A. Chapman and told him that I had traveled with a minister for nearly a year before attempting to preach. I had been advised this was the proper way to start. He replied, "When God calls a man he gives him a message." I took this to mean that if I was really called I could not have waited so long to start preaching.

At the called meeting Brother A. B. Peterman, a local elder, remarked, "Every young convert has a missionary spirit; he may take this for a call to the ministry." We were questioned, advised and allowed to proceed. Brother Peterman's remark bothered me till four years later, while I was assisting in a meeting at Albion, which he attended, Brother Peterman expressed to me his confidence in my ministry.

This campmeeting was attended by an Idaho farmer named Elmer Nichols who brought his wife, her sister, whose name was Mattie Cole, and another girl who worked for them named Rosa Brannon. All of these were saved and baptized in this meeting.

It was at this campmeeting that I received my first position with the church. I was the offical bell-ringer whose duty it was to ring the rising bell at 5:30 A.M. that people should arise and prepare for the morning prayer service which was held at 6:00 A.M. As I walked up and down the path ringing the bell one of these girls would peak at me from under her tent, taking care that I did not see her. I did not know this till years later when she had become Mrs. Gray.

This summer it was my privilege to attend also the campmeeting held at Ford's mill near Kippen, Idaho. This was a local meeting and not very largely attended, however it was quite effective. Some opposition was aroused. One man became angry and threatened to burn down the tent. Brother Walker said to him, "I would advise you to place a guard over this tent for if anything happens to it you will be held responsible." Nothing happened to the tent.

Another man opposed eating pork saying the devil is in the hog, that when the devils were cast out of the man in the tombs they entered the swine. To this Brother Peterman replied, "All those hogs were drowned, and still today the devil says, 'Away with the hogs'".

I spent part of the summer at Palouse where I helped build a barn for Brother Ike Turnbow. One day I was sharpening stakes with a hatchet and singing, "Do you triumph, Oh my brother," which has a slow movement. Brother J. C. Peterman, who heard me, called out, "Sing Zacchaeus Bold." This song has a rapid movement. I was of a slow, deliberate movement, seldom in a hurry.

During this period I preached a number of times for the church in Palouse. One of the members was a dentist, Dr. G. T. Henwood. Another was Mrs. Jennie Powers who employed Rosa Brannon as her house maid for a few years.

Late in the year my brother Will bought the Ideal Grocery on Monroe Street in Spokane. I clerked for him during the following winter and worshipped in the church at Spokane and did some gospel work in visiting the sick and praying with people.

On March 10th, 1906, Brothers John Murphy, Henry Maib and I went to Waukon, in the Big Bend country, to hold a meeting. This place was just a "whistle stop" where we were to be met. One of Frank Cole's daughters met us and took us to their home. The wind was blowing strong and cold as we left Spokane and became worse as we reached our destination. A snow storm soon blew up. We were to have services in the school house on Sunday where we spent most of the day but on account of the storm no one came. As the storm kept up for a few days we gave up the project and returned to Spokane.

As spring approached I became eager to be more active in the ministry. I told Will I would like to quit the store so he let me go as he would not hinder me in gospel work.

First I went to Creston to attend the campmeeting there. A number of the young people had pledged each other that they would not get saved in that meeting. Their resistance was so strong that the preaching seemed ineffective. Finally the Lord used Sister Ida Chapman to break through their stubborness and most if not all of them were saved.

The Colfax meeting followed soon after this. In this meeting there was much emphasis placed on social conduct. The discussion was carried into the young people's meetings. We were told to "Set your affections on things above, not on things on the earth." God will provide you a companion much as he did Isaac who went to the field to meditate (pray). He looked up and saw Rebekah coming to him. One young man arose and said, "I have no more need of a wife than a wagon has of five wheels." Others made similar statements. I said, "Perhaps in a few years I will want to marry but I am not at all interested at the present time." (I was twenty years of age.) Other boys made similar remarks but fortunately the girls kept still.

All such efforts to change or curb human nature were not very effective for one couple was married within two months and others followed not long after. How they ever became engaged is a deep secret.

During the campmeeting the foundation was laid for the new chapel building. I was among those who remained after the meeting to construct the building. I worked as a carpenter's helper and as a painter. We donated our work and received our board.

After a number of weeks harvest time came. Some of the boys took jobs in harvest and I went with them but after a few days I discovered I was no farmer so I returned to work in the chapel. Brother Forsyth, the foreman, offered to pay those who would come back $1.50 a day. I remained on the job till it was finished then gave back a part of my wages.

I accompanied Brothers Baldwin and T. W. Cooper in a meeting at Juliaetta, Idaho, where I did some of the preaching. I preached so long at one morning service that the people left one by one till none were left except our company. Brother Cooper exclaimed, "Thank God for a clean house." I learned since that I need not attempt to tell all I know in one sermon.

After this meeting I accompanied Brothers Peterman, Baldwin and Cooper in a meeting at Mohler, Idaho, a small community on Nez Perce prarie. The meeting was held at the home of Brother Hall and continued several days. Saints from surrounding communities came and attended the meeting. Day services were held for the saints and neighbors came at night.

As Brother Peterman was the only ordained minister of our group he did most of the preaching, but he refused to do it all.

30

He warned us that we must do our part and not depend on him to carry the load.

At the next service, after prayer, Brother Peterman arose and left the room. When time for preaching came he was still absent. We looked at each other till ashamed so I arose to preach. I had barely started to speak when Brother Peterman returned, grinning, and sat in the front seat facing me. I preached on the subject of Christian Perfection. After I had finished Brother Peterman sat me in the corner, both literally and figurately, and told me I had it wrong. I was unable to answer him, but I had heard his brother, A. B. Peterman, preach much as I had explained it. At the following Saints Home Assembly I overheard him discuss the matter with Brother J. L. Green, who explained it much as I had preached. Brother Peterman did not discuss the matter further with me.

In the fall of the year Brother Peterman moved to Moscow where he secured the Old Dunkard meetinghouse. A meeting was held there in December in which Brother H. A. Brooks, from Canada, assisted. I was present also. As the visiting minister Brother Brooks did most of the preaching though Brother Peterman helped. One night both of them sat still at preaching time so I arose and gave a message which was neither appropriate nor effective. Brother Peterman had felt the message but hesitated in deference to Brother Brooks.

It was while this meeting was going on that Brothers Brooks, Peterman and I visited Palouse where we ate a meal at the home of Sister Jennie Powers. Rosa Brannon, who worked for Sister Powers, waited table. I do not recall speaking to her. But on our way back to Moscow Brother Brooks asked me questions about Rosa. There was little that I could tell him and less that I cared to tell for I thought a stranger from Canada, who was older, had less right to be interested in her than I, and I was not interested, at least so my theology taught me. Thus ends another chapter in my ministry.

31

ITENERANT EVANGELISM

The year 1907 marks the beginning of a new epoch in my ministry, an epoch which lasted about ten years. Previous to this time I had preached here and there as opportunity was given without much plan or order. In 1905 I preached 19 times in six different places. In 1906 I preached 22 times in four places. But in 1907 I began the year in a "protracted" meeting in which I took a leading part. Such meetings often continued ten days, two weeks, or even a month. I have preached three times on Sunday, taught two Sunday School classes and rode eight miles on horseback. In those ten years I preached in no less than fifty places within a radius of one hundred miles of Lewiston, Idaho. I proceed to tell of some of these meetings.

The Saints Home Assembly, November, 1906, was attended by an elderly gentleman named John Holingsworth who lived on Cream Ridge near Lenore, Idaho. The family of W. S. Wade, formerly of Spokane, lived in the same neighborhood. These people arranged with Brother J. C. Peterman for a meeting to be held at Cream Ridge in January. For some reason Brother Peterman could not go so he sent Brother Baldwin and me in his stead. Brother B. V. George, Brother Baldwin's brother-in-law, came with us. Although Brother Peterman's inability to come was a disappointment we received good cooperation.

We began preaching various doctrines such as Christ's Mission, God's Sheep, The Church, Freedom from Sin, and the New Birth. We gave no altar call till the 14th night. That night I preached on Repentance, intending to give an altar call. But without waiting a lady arose and said, "I want to get saved, I can't wait any longer." From that night on some were saved nearly every night.

The effects of this meeting were felt throughout the area. Formerly there was a dance every Saturday night. After this it was two years before the dances were revived. Some of those saved have remained stalwart in the church for more than fifty years and the grandchildren of others are with us.

After this meeting was over Brother George and I divided our time with this young church and the one at Orofino for several weeks. Although I did most of the preaching Brother George preached some also. One Sunday morning I had no message and felt sure God had given Brother George the message. When time for preaching came we both waited, then I stood up hoping the Lord would put words into my mouth, as he has sometimes, but I could not think of any words to say. I turned to Brother George and said, "Brother George I know God has given you the message, get up here and preach it." He arose and preached a good sermon.

When spring came arrangements were made to hold a tent meeting in Lenore. A number of people came and camped to attend the meeting. Brother Peterman and Brother S. P. McCully were both present and they did the preaching. I preached only once. It was a very good meeting.

One man who had a very peculiar spirit told us his story. He was a hard sinner as he attended a revival meeting. He started to leave the service but as he reached the door he fell to the floor where he writhed helplessly, then got up shouting. That night the devil visited him. There was quite a struggle then he took a bad choking spell. The next he knew the devil was gone. Brother McCully asked, "Do you know where he went? he went right down your throat." If Brother McCully was right it was not the first time he had made a correct diagnosis.

Shortly after the tent meeting Brother George and I decided to start a Sunday School and meetings at Lenore. We were told that the store-keeper was a religious man so we sought his help. He tried to discourage us by pointing out that we would need so many officers—a superintendent, assistant-superintendent, secretary, teachers and officers and there were not enough religious people in the area to run a Sunday School. But we went on without him and announced Sunday School. Forty people came out. We did not bother to organize but we divided them into two classes and I taught one class and he the other. Then we preached to them. The enterprise did not succeed because soon an epidemic of diphtheria broke out which required us to discontinue.

As my folks lived in Spokane I liked to go home occasionally. I found that Brothers G. W. Bailey and S. H. Eddings were to hold a tent meeting at Deer Park, north of Spokane, so I accompanied them. I was not responsible for this meeting and spoke only once.

The church at Spokane burned wood for heating purposes. A man who owned a tract of wood near Penrith, Washington, offered the church a car load of wood if they would cut it. I was with a group who went to cut the wood. But I was asked to assist with the cooking to feed the men. Also we had religious services and I preached.

But I could not remain long from my field of labor. Although we sought to get the message to as many new people as possible we did not neglect the new converts. So with Brothers Baldwin and George we visited the little groups and isolated members on Craig Mountain, mostly on foot. One morning we stood in the road trying to decide where to go next. I said, "I feel led to go to Orofino," but both of them said they did not feel that way but for me to go if I thought I should. My feelings were strong so I started alone.

The sky was overcast and the air was perfectly still. I started down the road toward Lenore where I would take the train. It soon began to rain, not the kind of shower that sends the chickens scurrying for cover but the kind when hens stay out in it all day. The road was graded but not graveled. Soon my feet were very muddy and I was getting wet, but I was on my way.

I trudged on till I reached Gifford; there on the sidewalk I saw Brother Wade. His buggy had broken so he left it in the blacksmith shop to be fixed. He took me to the restaurant for a meal then took me home with him. I would not say the Lord broke his buggy so he would have to wait for me but anyway the

Lord made use of his accident to furnish me a ride out of the rain. I went home with Brother Wade and later took the train to Orofino.

Upon arriving at Orofino I visited Brother Alteneder. Always when a minister arrives arrangements are made for meetings. Up Orofino Creek near the mouth of Whiskey Creek lived a family named Hunt. Mrs. Hunt was a good Christian, and so was their young daughter, but Mr. Hunt and other relatives were unsaved. Living with them was Mrs. Hunt's sister who was bedfast with TB. It was decided to hold the services at the Hunt home.

At the first service there were about twenty people present. These consisted of the Hunts with some of their relatives, a few neighbors and saints. While I was preaching Mrs. Dunlap, the lady with TB, gave a screaching cry which sent a shiver up my spine. She assumed to be praising God but it was the wrong spirit. At the close of the meeting Brother Alteneder said to me, "That woman is devil possessed." I thought so too. The story of her deliverance will be told elsewhere. After a few days Brother George came and remained with me for the remainder of the meeting. One night every sinner present, except two men, was saved.

There were two incidents in this meeting I wish to tell. One was that of a young man who was seeking sanctification. He was kneeling at a chair as we prayed for him. Suddenly he fell over and struck his elbow on the floor. In a moment he arose his face aglow with joy.

Another case was that of a neighbor lady who came under deep conviction and while kneeling she was calling aloud for salvation. Her husband, a wicked sinner, took her by the arm and said, "Come on old lady, we are going home now," but she kept on praying. Brother George and I rebuked him and commanded him to leave her alone. He looked frightened and left the house. In a moment he opened the door and called to her, "Old lady, you need not come home at all now." So that night she went home with neighbors. After the man had gone home we heard a gun shot. Some thought he had committed suicide or was attempting to frighten his wife. After a day or two he came for her and took her home. Then he met me on the road and gave me the worst cursing I ever heard a man received but it did not ruffle me a bit. I rejoiced in my heart that I was a child of God. The night this man came to meeting he was followed by his pet pig. Someone remarked that he thought the man and the pig had kindred spirits.

For several years a ten-day Assembly was held at Moscow at the New Year season with three sermons a day. In January of 1908 a request came for prayer for the healing of a lady at Asotin. The story of her healing will be found elsewhere. She requested that we come to Asotin for a meeting so in May Brother and Sister Baldwin, Brother Ray Nichols, Brother C. R. Little, a layman, and I went to Asotin to hold a meeting. We supposed a place to hold the meeting had been found but upon our arrival we found that no arrangements had been made.

It was only recently that we had found ourselves unwelcome in a Lutheran church due to the things we preached so we thought we would try to secure the school house where we would be more free. But the school board objected that the seats were not suitable for such use and as there were five churches in town and only two of them had pastors we should be able to get one of them.

We first approached a deacon of the Baptist church. He showed interest but said we should see a trustee to get permission to use the church and told us where he lived. The trustee was not at home but his wife was eager for us to have the meeting and said she was sure her husband would give his consent if he were home. She sent us back to the deacon to get the key. But the deacon refused to give us the key without consent of the trustee himself. We learned he was in Coeur d'Alene in northern Idaho and hard to reach. The other trustees were dead or their terms had expired, so we had reached a dead end so far as the Baptist church was concerned.

We next attempted to secure the Christian church. The member whom we approached asked what we would preach. Brother Baldwin replied, Salvation, sanctification, divine healing and unity." The man answered that there is no such thing as divine healing and they did not want such stuff taught in their church. The amazing thing about it all was that he was the husband of the lady who had sent for us and he knew she had been healed but refused to believe it anyway.

We next tried the United Brethren church. As they had no pastor we approached the Sunday School superintendent. He was very favorable and would have let us have the church if he had the authority but he offered to help us any way that he could. We did not try the Methodist church or the Presbyterian church as they each had a pastor.

Though we found no building in which to preach we were eager to have meetings anyway. Brother Baldwin and I walked down the road looking for an opening. We saw a man working in his garden so talked with him. Brother Baldwin poured out the gospel on him but he just listened and would not talk. His wife saw us and called, "Daddy, come in, supper is ready," but he paid no heed. We kept on talking so soon again the wife called, "Daddy, bring me some wood to finish cooking supper," but again he paid no heed. Brother Baldwin kept on pouring out the truth. Again his wife called, "Daddy, don't let those men sell you something you don't want." Brother Baldwin shouted back, "Maybe he wants salvation." She answered, "What is that?" Brother Baldwin replied, "Maybe he wants to get saved." The lady answered, "If that is what you are talking about I know something about that," and came out where we were. We told her we were looking for a place to have meeting. She said, "You can have meeting in our house, can't they, can't they Daddy?" But the old man answered not a word, so we knew we were not welcome. Then the woman told us that the folks in the big house across the street were good Christians and would welcome us so we tried there but the parents were not at home.

Though we found no place in which to have meeting there remained the great outdoors. Our company gathered outside and sang lustily for quite a while and I am sure many people heard us. We had come to Asotin to have meeting and had no intention of giving up or of being stopped by the devil or by men. We surveyed our resources to see what we could do or might do and came up with a plan. It did not look promising or even sensible but we decided to see it through. We would have a tent meeting; but where was the tent? You shall see.

In coming to Asotin we brought along our personal effects such as our clothing, bedding and a tent to sleep in. The tent was 10' x 12'. We decided to make other sleeping arrangements and to use the tent for meeting. We borrowed some boards and blocks of wood to make seats and spread our bedding on the boards to make softer seats. We secured a barrel and draped it with Sister Baldwin's apron for a pulpit and had a coal oil lantern for light. We sent two girls down the streets to invite people to the tent meeting on the hill near the school. Probably a dozen people came looking for the tent. We went inside and sang and prayed and preached while the people stood outside and listened.

Then we secured another tent 12 x 14 and placed the two tents facing each other with a space between covered by a tarpaulin. Then our U. B. friend came to our rescue and loaned us 40 chairs. Soon people began to come and we had good attendance and were well received. The wife of the Baptist trustee was interested and I think received a real blessing. Our U. B. friend accepted our message and took his stand with us. The last I knew of him he and his family were standing true to the movement. But the husband of the woman who had been healed and who sent for us withstood us to the end. We were unable to reach him but it may be that God has done so since.

This experience impressed us with the need of a gospel tent so a number of brethren in Idaho joined together and bought a tent 18 x 30 which was to be used in gospel work in Idaho. This

38

tent was used several years and was in charge of Brother Baldwin.

The first place where this tent was used was at Spalding, Idaho, about ten miles east of Lewiston. This is the oldest settlement in Idaho where Henry Spalding, the missionary, is buried.

In the summer of 1908 a young lady and a girl drove up a mountain road called Coyote Grade. As they reached a cabin they stopped their buggy and left a copy of the Gospel Trumpet at the gate. When they had driven on the lady of the house sent a child out to bring in the paper. After reading it she was so well pleased that she wrote the editor asking that a minister be sent their way to preach to them. The request was sent to Brother Baldwin so he and I and some others went to Spalding and conducted a tent meeting. The attendance was not large, as it was a small town, but several were saved and remained true till death.

After I had preached a sermon on sanctification Brother Kirk, who had just been saved, said this might be good for some people but he was fully satisfied and could not hold any more. But on Sunday morning he drove up this grade to do his chores and was in a hurry to get back to the meeting. But his horses balked on the grade and began to back in danger of running off the road. He became very excited and angry. When he returned he said he could see that he did need something more.

One lady came to the altar to get saved. When she had prayed through to victory she raised her hand in praise. Suddenly she took it down and raised the other arm. Then I noticed she had a ring on her first hand. We had said nothing about rings.

Old Brother Stubbs gave up his tobacco. The next day I visited the home and saw some cigars in a glass on the center table. He saw me looking at them and said he had left them there to tempt the devil with. But the devil turned the tables and the next day he smoked one. He learned the devil is not to be played with.

We had some opposition from a rough element but on the whole we had a very successful meeting.

At the close of the meeting there were some to be baptized, but as I was not ordained I did not know whether I should baptize. I wrote Brother Bailey about it and he replied that the commission to preach includes to baptize so we had baptism in the Clearwater River. The first person I baptized was Brother Kirk. I thought I would have to hold him well to keep him from going to the bottom but instead I did not get quite all of his hair under. For many years after this he and his wife (the lady who first sent for us) were with the Gilbert church at Portland.

Sometime later I held a meeting in the school house at Spalding. One night I chanced to remark that the pope does not profess to live free from sin. This angered the Catholics who threatened to drive me out of town. The next night I confirmed my statement with a quotation from Cardinal Gibbon's Faith of Our Fathers. The opposition became so strong, throwing stones at the building and the attendants, that we had a deputy sheriff come to protect us. Then the opposition ceased.

There were ten people converted in the meeting. We did very little to organize the group except that I would return at times and preach for them. The Methodist Presiding Elder thought it would be a good time to organize a Methodist church so he sent a preacher there for that purpose. He canvassed the town and persuaded six of my ten converts to agree to join his church which he would organize the next Sunday. I knew nothing of this when I went to Spalding to preach Friday and Saturday nights. Saturday night I preached on the Scattering and Gathering of God's Sheep. The preacher was present so I asked him if I might use him and his church for illustration, to which he agreed. As I preached I described the very things he had been doing the past few days although as yet I knew nothing of it. It seems the Lord directed me as to what to say.

In my sermon I pointed out that there is but one fold and one Shepherd, that we become members of the fold through being saved, and this fold contains all true Christians and no sinners. I then showed how hireling false shepherds divide and scatter the flock by coaxing them into their own pens. Then I told how the Lord is now gathering his sheep back into the one fold destroying sectarian division.

The preacher frequently said "Amen," then turned his head and tried to laugh it off. At the close of the service he came to me quite angry and said, "Tonight you have wiped the Methodist church off the face of the earth." I replied, "If a little fellow like me can destroy your church you had better get out of it and get into the church that the gates of hell cannot prevail against."

As a result of this meeting my six converts, and perhaps some others, backed out and refused to join his church. So he gave up the project and did not try to organize his church on Sunday as he had planned.

At a later time we held another tent meeting in Spalding. The opposition was not so great this time but there was some. One night someone threw a cat under the tent wall but the cat showed us the respect of walking out quitely without showing any disturbance. On another night someone tried to direct the water of an irrigation ditch into the tent but the water turned and went in another direction.

Results of these meetings continue. For some time a Sunday School was conducted in the School house with occasional preaching services. Descendents of these converts are carrying on the work of the Lord if not there elsewhere.

The year 1908 was important in another way also for in February a Ministerial Assembly was held in Portland in the new Missionary Home on Hawthorne Boulevard. It was attended by ministers from California, Oregon, Washington and Idaho, about fifty in all. The meeting got off to a slow start waiting for Brother John L. Green to arrive. When he arrived he had some matters to present to the ministers for our consideration. His main topic was spiritual gifts which he discussed at great length. Briefly stated his view was that through the complete consecration of the individual the Holy Spirit takes full control and uses the natural abilities and faculties of the person. To illustrate his theory he asked Brother Bamford to yield fully his hand, giving him a piece of chalk. He then took Brother Bamford's hand and wrote the letter "J". But the letter did not look quite like the handwriting of either. The explanation was the hand was not fully yielded.

As another demonstration Brother Green had Brother Van Laanan speak in the Holland language, then interpret what he said into English. Brother Green said the first was the gift of tongues, the brother speaking under the inspiration of the Spirit, and then the gift of interpretation.

Most of the brethren could not agree and one said, "It is as clear as mud." Brother Green told us he was not preaching this publicly but was giving it to us for our consideration. But soon some were saying that a bad heresy was brewing and developing and that we must resist it. I had not taken a stand against Brother Green neither had I endorsed his doctrine but the story got around that I had a "Green spirit," and a "Green devil" had been cast out of me, all of which was untrue. Brothers E. E. Byrum and D. O. Teasley came and cleared the matter up for us. Brother Green humbly yielded.

LOVE AND MARRIAGE

The year 1909 proved to be a very important period in my life. In January of that year the usual Assembly at Moscow was held. I did my share of preaching, Brother Baldwin and Brother G. W. Bailey were also present and preaching.

The church building at Moscow was so constructed that the ground floor was used as the parsonage and the upper floor as the auditorium. On January 15th, after the morning service, I went to the parsonage and there I saw Rosa Brannon. Though I had known her for sometime it was about two years since I had seen her. She had spent Christmas with her family who lived near Troy. She had come to Moscow to attend the Assembly.

My mother had come from Spokane to see me and to visit her brother (Brother Baldwin) and to attend the meeting. She saw

Rosa and said to me, "You want to get that girl." I made no reply but I thought it was not a bad idea. Though Rosa and I saw each other at meeting every day we never had a private conversation with each other.

After the Moscow Assembly concluded Brother Olson, who lived not far from Pullman, asked us to hold a meeting at the school near where he lived. Brother Baldwin and I went and took turn about preaching. Rosa and Ethel Doyle came along to assist in the singing and whatever else they might do. Ethel Doyle was a young married woman whose husband was away from home at that time. Rosa stayed with her while in Moscow. Although we were thrown together at every meal and every service I had no private conversation with either lady. The attendance at the meeting was not large and although the preaching was good the permanent results were small.

After the close of the meeting Brother Olson took Rosa and me back to Pullman. I think the others had gone already. We rode in Brother Olson's hack with Brother Olson and Rosa in the seat while I sat on a trunk in the back. The weather was cold with a wind blowing. Rosa's cheeks were red from the wind. It was then that I really noticed how beautiful she was.

After returning to Moscow I wrote some music and took it to Ethel to ask her to play it for me. When Rosa saw me coming she left the room. I asked Ethel to call her back as I wanted her opinion also on my music. Really I wanted her presence more than her opinion. I was beginning to become interested in her.

A group of our people living in and near Troy desired a meeting at that place. They secured a building and sent for us. Brothers Baldwin and Cooper and I went. Brothers George and Rawie were present also part of the time. Although Rosa's family lived near Troy she spent most of her time at the meeting and helped in the work of feeding the preachers.

It was common practice those days for the saints to carry a notebook in which they recorded the scriptures used by the preacher. Through some means I learned that Rosa's book was full (I still have it) so I bought a new one and gave it to her. This was the first present I ever gave her.

The revival was quite successful though it stirred considerable controversy in the town. We left a small congregation and I came from Moscow frequently to preach to them until they secured a pastor.

It was during one of these trips that I became aware that I was deeply in love with Rosa. But the big problem was how to let her know and how to find out how she felt.

It was on the 18th of March that Brother William A. Hunnex came to Moscow to give a lecture on China before his return to that country to head our missionary work among the Chinese people. He was a good friend of Brother Baldwin so stopped to visit him.

There is an interesting and important story connected with their friendship. I received the information partly from Brother Hunnex and partly from Brother Baldwin.

Brother Hunnex was born of missionary parents in China and was a British subject. He had come to the United States and while in North Dakota he gave lectures on China at various small towns in the Red River Valley. Having completed his itinerary he came to Grand Forks and found the church of God camp-meeting in progress. So, having no other lectures scheduled, he attended the campmeeting.

An incident occurred that came near affecting his whole life and our Chinese missionary work. It was like this: Brother Hunnex took quite an interest in the children and played with them. This would not have been objectionable, but he played with them on Sunday. For this he received a severe reprimand by one of the ministers. He was greatly offended and left the campground.

When Brother Baldwin learned about it he rode his bicycle to the railroad station where he found Brother Hunnex waiting for a train to leave town. Brother Baldwin persuaded him to return to

44

the campmeeting where he was fully won to the truth. Later he spent some time at the New York Missionary Home.

This visit to Moscow took place on my birthday. Rosa was visiting Sister Baldwin that day so she baked a cake, partly for Brother Hunnex but I was included in the honors. This was the first but not the last cake Rosa made for me.

Rosa had returned to Moscow and accepted employment with Mrs. Shields on North Adams Street as house maid. I made my home while in Moscow with Brother Baldwin. One Friday, April 2nd, I was out in the back yard cutting wood with a buck saw. I always considered a buck saw and a saw buck my worst enemies. A sudden squall of tapioca snow gave me excuse for going into the house. There I found that the mail had left a letter for Rosa Brannon. I thought it would be a friendly act to take it to her and also that might open the way for me to tell her how I felt.

When I reached the house she came to the door. I told her I had some mail for her. She opened the screen, received the mail and closed the screen, thanking me for it. I hesitated a moment, then turned on my heel and left.

The next day some more mail came so I tried it again. Again she received the mail, thanked me, and closed the screen. But I did not leave immediately, my courage arose and I said, "Sister Rosa, somehow I feel the Lord is drawing our hearts together." She replied, "I have been feeling the same way." I said, "Let us pray earnestly about it," then turned and went away.

That afternoon I took the train for Troy where I was to preach the next day. The train had not left the city limits before an imp climbed on my right shoulder and said, "You silly gump, Rosa meant she thought you were getting soft toward her, she don't care for you." I had to resist the devil to drive the imp away.

I think I preached unusually well that Sunday for I was on the mountain top. Then I returned to Moscow. I called on Rosa again on April 7th without the need of mail to go. This time she invited me in. We talked though not on the all important subject. But I made an appointment to come back on the 9th.

On April 9th Rosa met me at the door clothed in a beautiful gingham dress well starched and ironed. We talked a while and I asked her if she had reached a decision concerning marriage and she said she had and she would marry me. I understood it was the bride's privilege to set the date. If she had said next week, or tomorrow, that would have been agreeable with me. She suggested some time in June. She must have a wedding dress made and a few other things done. So it was to be sometime in June.

While I was in Moscow I would visit Rosa frequently. Mrs. Shields soon discovered why I was coming and had Rosa entertain me in the small parlor. A close friend of Rosa's worked for the lady next door. Mrs. Shields invited the girl over then they watched us through the window, then tapping on the window to let us know we were seen. Rosa tried to get her girl friend not to tell that I was visiting her but it is very hard to keep such secrets without help.

During the waiting period I went to Stites to hold some meetings and spent part of the time at the home of Brother Howard who knew our early preachers in Pennsylvania. Sister Howard told me I reminded her of Brother Kilpatrick who, when he was at their house, spent much time writing sermons. What she did not know was that I was writing nine page letters to the girl I loved. In order to keep the matter secret I would walk to town, four miles, to mail my letters and to receive hers. Why did we want to keep it secret? I don't really know. Nowadays an engagement ring advertises the fact. In those days rings were not used among us.

One day while visiting Rosa I asked her for a kiss. She said, "I don't know what the saints think about that." But I said that since we were engaged it would be all right. She accepted my view. I had never kissed a girl before. That was the sweetest kiss. I had practiced greeting the brethren with the holy kiss but this was different. There had never been one like this and I am sure none was ever more holy.

In a short time Rosa gave up her job and went home to make ready for the wedding. I still went to Troy for Sunday services. One Sunday a brother offered to buy me a ticket back to Moscow but I explained that I had clergy rates and could buy cheaper than he could and I would rather buy my own. But my real reason was that I did not plan to go back to Moscow but would get off the train at Howell, a little cross road stop, which I did. I walked up the road about a mile which brought me to the Brannon gate where Rosa met me. I spent a few days visiting her parents and her sisters. They liked me well enough to approve our marriage.

After this I assisted in a tent meeting at Albion, Washington, which is between Pullman and Colfax. An evangelist for a certain denomination had held a meeting just previous to our coming. He was to be paid according to the number of converts he could secure. He had secured nearly one hundred confessions so he remained a few days after the meeting closed hoping to reach that goal and receive extra pay, but he failed.

I left before our meeting closed as I wanted to get to Spokane to prepare for our wedding. I sold my bicycle, it was not made for two, for fifteen dollars. I put another dollar with it and bought my wedding suit. I proceeded to Spokane, Rosa was to come later.

The Spokane campmeeting was in progress. Someone had heard of our plan to get married so arose in testimony meeting and said, "People should not think about getting married during campmeeting but should be praying for souls." The minister said, "There will be no weddings during campmeeting."

By this time Rosa had arrived and wanted to attend the meeting but wanted to be married first. I had attended all the services except when I went to town to get our license. I explained our situation to Brother Bailey who agreed to marry us in a private ceremony after the night service so on Thursday night, June 17th,

1909, we were married in my brother Will's home in the presence of several of my relatives and some of Rosa's friends. I had gone to meeting that night as usual and remained through the altar service and Rosa had taken a nap while waiting.

The next morning we went to the campmeeting and surprised many of the people. I used Paul's argument that I had as much right to lead about a wife as others had.

After this campmeeting we attended the Colfax campmeeting but our real honeymoon included a trip to Seattle where we attended the campmeeting there.

We remained in the Puget Sound area for the rest of the summer where we helped Brother J. C. Peterman in a meeting at Puyallup and at Orting. After this we were in a tent meeting at Parkland with Brother George Burgess. When this meeting closed we remained at Parkland and set up housekeeping. On the back part of a lot owned by Brother Burgess was a building 10 x 12 which was intended for a garage or wood shed. He permitted us to use it for living and cooking while we slept in a tent. We borrowed some dishes and bought a cookstove for $1.00 and bought a few other things till we had only five cents left of the $2.35 we had to begin with. I spent this last nickle for a loaf of bread. But I might have saved it for the Lord put in into the heart of a neighbor lady, a stranger, to bring us a loaf of home baked bread fresh from the oven. We had bread, jelly and water to start with, with the joy of the Lord.

We spent several weeks at Parkland not knowing where our next dollar would come from but some way the Lord provided. We never went hungry and while our needs were supplied there never was a surplus.

After some weeks a gentleman at Puyallup had us come to his home to care for their children while he and his wife went to eastern Washington to dispose of their grain crop. He gave us $5.00 and promised more when his crop would be sold. We are not sure that it has been sold yet.

As fall approached our friends in Idaho urged us to return so we decided to do so. We had a little less than enough money to pay our train fare to Spokane. Sister Peterman sold milk. She went with us to the depot and on the way collected $1.00 from one of her customers and gave it to us. This enabled us to buy our tickets. At Spokane we were among friends.

In November we attended the Assembly Meeting at Colfax. I had preached for nearly five years but had not preached at the Colfax camp—or assembly meetings. My converts would ask me, "Why don't you preach? You can preach better than any who have preached yet." I thought they were prejudiced but I did preach once at this meeting.

At the closing day of the Assembly it was planned to have an ordination service. Brothers T. W. Cooper and W. J. Baldwin and Sister Pearl McCarter were to be ordained. At time for the service to begin Brother S. P. McCully said, "There is Fred Gray, he should be ordained too." The other ministers agreed so, along with these others, I was ordained on November 28, 1909.

This was the last Assembly held at Colfax and thereafter the fall meeting was held in Spokane though the summer camp-meeting continued to be held at Colfax.

Early in January, 1910, Rosa and I went to the town of Colfax, the home of the Chapmans and the Coopers, to assist in a meeting. One night I preached on the return of Christ. Sister Chapman was much impressed and said she would preach more frequently on that subject in the future.

I suppose I dream every night but seldom am I impressed with them. But in this meeting I had an impressive dream. There was a field of ripe grain. Brother Cooper and I were using binders to reap the grain. We were instructed to finish the field before sundown and it was now afternoon. There was a small patch of unripe grain and a slough we were to leave and cut only the ripe grain. As the day wore away we hurried our horses more and more till we had them running. We completed the field just as the sun went down. The dream impressed me that we must hasten with the Lord's work for the time is short.

Soon after this Rosa and I went back to Peck, Idaho, to hold a meeting. The services were held in the Methodist church. The meeting got off to a good start. The pastor gave us his blessing and the people were quite receptive. I was very sorry we could not continue the meeting.

It so happened that the church at Troy planned a meeting at the same time and had secured from me a tentative promise to **hold it for them.** But I learned they were trying to secure Brother W. W. Crist so went to Peck. But when it was known that Brother Crist could not come they telephoned me that they had already rented the building for a month and wanted me to come at once to hold the meeting. Regretfully I closed the meeting at Peck to go to Troy. Though the meeting at Peck was short it may have had some effect for eventally the minister cast his lot with us.

At Troy I met a new situation. In the meeting held the previous year there was considerable doctrinal preaching on the church, divine healing and the evils of sectism. This aroused quite a lot of prejudice and opposition. This time, the church told me, they wanted only evangelistic preaching with no doctrine. Consequently I preached for a whole month on such subjects as repentance, when to get saved, the danger of neglect, etc. I was forced to prepare some new sermons which was good for me.

Usually the attendance was fair though one night only one outsider was present. When he came in he removed his overcoat and took a seat near the middle of the room as if he were settled for the night. So I aimed my sermon at him. When I got well under way he quietly arose, took his coat, and walked out. This left me in the middle of my sermon with only saints to preach to so I stumbled around for a while till, fortunately, another stranger came in and I finished up on him.

The hall was a one story building with a metal roof. There had been heavy snow but the weather had turned warm and rain had come. One night, with the crowd about half saints and half sinners, I preached on the coming of Christ, suddenly and unexpectedly. Suddenly there came a terrible noise like something coming right through the roof. Every sinner sprang to his feet but all the saints remained seated. A large pile of snow slid down the roof. This illustrated my sermon though I did not plan it.

On the last Sunday I broke the rule and preached a doctrinal sermon which was well appreciated. But on the whole the meeting was not a success. There were two professed conversions, both weak. I decided that never again will I permit the church to tell me what I may preach and what I may not preach.

Shortly after the meeting at Troy I returned to Stites. Rosa did not accompany me on this trip. A year before I had visited Brother Howard who lived near Stites at which time we held a few meetings in the Pleasant Valley school house. Brother George had conducted a few services there previously also so that a start had been made. By the end of the meeting of whcih I am now writing there was a substantial group of reliable people saved and baptised.

At one of the services I said something like this,, "We are not blaming you who are not saved; you need to hear the gospel first that you may know how to get saved: we are here to preach it to you." What I did not know was that a Baptist preacher was present in the audience. At the close of the service he challenged me telling me that he had preached frequently to these people. I apologized as I had not known that. As we conversed I asked him if he preached deliverance from sin to which he replied that no one can live above sin. I replied, "Then I was right when I assumed that these people had not heard the gospel."

After I preached a sermon on restitution this preacher's son told me that is not the way his father preaches but when God forgives you that settles everything. I said to him, "Suppose I had cheated you out of $5.00, then gone to your father's altar and prayed for forgiveness; then arose and praised the Lord for forgiveness: would you be satisfied? or would you want your money back?" He said, "I would want my money back."

One man who was happily saved went to his neighbor with whom he had quarreled and asked forgiveness. The neighbor forgave and said, "I was saved too once but I lost it." The new convert replied, "If you had what I have you couldn't lose it." But he was too sure of himself as he soon learned.

While we were in this general area we held a short meeting at the small town of Clearwater. A "holy-roller" preacher was in the area also. Sometimes while his service was going on he would fall over and lie on the floor while his wife sang and played on her guitar. He would say, "If I have a fit don't fear, it is a holy fit." He was not well received.

At our meeting one night I felt led to preach on the church. A minister and a deacon came in. I began to fear them but the Lord gave me courage. At the close of the service the deacon gave me a dollar. He was a good man and the Lord rewarded him by making a church of God preacher out of his son.

Brother Howard lived four miles up the Clearwater River from Stites, the end of the railroad. Six miles farther was the town of Harpster. This was a rest stop for travelers from Stites and from Grangeville going into the mining area at Elk City. Someone had asked for me to hold a meeting at Harpster. So far as I know no church of God minister had ever preached there. I knew no one, not even anyone's name.

I walked the six miles from Brother Howard's place carrying my grip with what little was in it. I arrived shortly before dark and learned the school was open. Consent had been received for me to hold a meeting there. As it became dark I lit the coal oil lamps and rang the school bell. After ringing it the second time a few junior boys came to learn what was going on. It seems the meeting had not been announced. I decided to preach to the boys, but as I began one man came in. I sang, prayed and preached just as if the house were full.

At the close of the service the man invited me home with him. Of course I went for I had no other plans except to sleep in the school house.

When news about the meeting got spread around the attendance increased so that by Sunday we had a large crowd. Sunday morning I felt led to preach on sanctification. I learned that there were Methodists present. I introduced my subject something like this, "This morning I wish to preach on sanctification. Some of you may say this is a Methodist sermon. It is true that John Wesley preached this. I preach it, not because he did but because it is in the Word of God. That is why he preached it, and that is why I preach it." At the close of the service a lady said to me, "That was a good Methodist sermon." But a man said, "I have heard the Methodists preach many times and I never heard them preach like that."

A short time after the meeting at Harpster closed I was to return to preach on Sunday. Rather than walking the six miles each way Brother Howard arranged for me to go horseback. His horses were away in pasture so he borrowed a horse from his close Indian neighbor. I was afraid to ride an Indian cayuse so Brother Howard fixed the bridle with a very severe spade bit. I had heard the way to keep a horse from throwing you is not to let him get his head down, so I drew the reins tight as I mounted. The horse reared on his hind legs. I thought he planned to throw me into the picket fence so I pulled harder. The horse fell over backwards, and stuck the saddle horn in the ground right beside me. He rolled over, got up, and so did I. I was not hurt but could have been killed. Then Brother Howard changed the bit and I rode the plow horse to Harpster and preached as planned.

The Lord blessed Brother and Sister Adams who opened their home to me by opening their hearts to the truth which they embraced and held so long as I knew them.

I will now relate some incidents that occurred in the town of Stites though some of them happened a few years later.

Our friends at Pleasant Valley were eager to have a meeting in Stites. They rented Packer's hall which was sometimes used as a theater. Here we had an extended meeting. Several of the leading people of the community, including the newspaper editor, were impressed with our message. There was much preaching on doctrine and our message was well received.

However someone objected that I was trying to get people to leave their churches to join mine. One night I challenged the crowd like this, "Which of you have I asked, either privately or publicly, to leave your church, will you stand?" No one stood. I then asked, "How many of you can see by the word of God which I have preached that there is only one church for all Christians and are willing to leave all that divided us that we all may be one, will you stand?" About two-thirds of the congregation arose. A nice local group was formed.

Some Baptists said they could trace their church back to their founder John, the Baptist. I replied, "John was a great prophet, but he was to prepare the way for Christ who was to increase while John was to decrease. One day John, with two of his disciples, saw Christ. John pointed him out and the disciples left John to follow Christ. If John were here today he would advise you to leave him to follow the deeper truths of Christ which we are preaching." Some Baptists followed this advice.

Numerous people were baptized, among them A. J. Stuart with his wife, his two sons and two daughters, and their dog followed them into the river. From this area the church of God has received five ministers, A. P. Gregory, Grace Kole, A. J. Stuart, E. V. and Edith Swinehart. Also A. A. Howard was returned to the ministry.

While we were in Stites a lady informed us that in Grangeville there was a group of about twenty people who were reading the Gospel Trumpet and holding prayer meetings. She was sure they would welcome a meeting by us. Brother A. J. Stuart accompanied me as we went to Grangeville where we found this group and held a meeting with them.

Though these people readily accepted the doctrinal truths, especially about the church, and were quite united in heart they had many intellectual differences due to different backgrounds.

They were from the following faiths: Catholic, Lutheran, Adventist, Baptist, Christian Church, Mormon, Church of Christ, Penticostal and Christian Catholic Apostolic Church in Zion (Dowietite). Also there were a few with no former religion.

These all got along very well during the meeting but after I had gone their differences caused some confusion, so they sent for me to come back. I proposed that I take up their particular views one by one and compare them with the word of God. They all said that is what they would like, so I proceeded.

First of all I took up the peculiar views of Dr. Dowie. A man and his wife were of this teaching. First I stated Dowie's views which they agreed was a correct statement. Then I proceeded to point out his errors. The lady took it alright but the man got angry. Then I dealt with other doctrines in like manner. I think much good was done.

At one prayermeeting a lady was praying for sanctification when she received a great blessing. Even the Pentecostal lady agreed that this lady was baptized with the Holy Spirit for she heard her speak in a tongue, she stammered while praying. This is the "stammering tongue" the Bible speaks about!

Brother John Hollingsworth (We called him Uncle Johnny), an elderly gentleman, frequently accompanied me in evangelistic work. He was with us at Grangeville and was helpful in prayer, testimony and exhortation. We would visit together. We visited the lady who had been a Catholic and as we were about to leave she fell on her knees before me and cried, "Bless me, Father, Bless me." We prayed with her and her face lightened up, God really blessed her.

Toward the close of the meeting we had a baptismal service in which several were baptised, among them two young ladies, daughters of an army officer. They had never professed before and did not know how to pray. Uncle Johnny taught them to repent.

The Methodists and the Presbyterians had gone together to form the Federated Church. One of their ladies often came to our meetings and would remind us that she belonged to the "Methodist wing of the Federated Church." As the Methodist church building was not in use our folks rented it for a nominal sum.

Our group included a former member of the Church of Christ. He informed me that he had been a deacon and implied that he was willing to accept a place of leadership. However the congregation asked Brother C. K. Chapman to become their pastor. They voted to pay him $40.00 a month though no individual pledges were taken. A few gave a dollar each but the total raised fell short. So Brother Chapman had to work to help support his family. However the same situation existed most everywhere among our churches. I knew of only one church in our whole area that supported its pastor.

Now that the church was in the capable hands of Brother Chapman I felt relieved of responsibility for them.

The events just related reach somewhat beyond the year 1910 to which I now return. After spending some time at and about Stites I returned to Troy for a short while before the Colfax campmeeting which we always attended.

It had now become evident that we needed a home of our own. I borrowed $200.00 and bought a lot in Juliaetta for $150.00 on which I built our house of four rooms 7 x 9 each. The entire cost of the house was $50.15. I bought dimension lumber for $10.00 per M and shiplap for $11.00 per M. The two doors were given to me but all else I bought. I did all the work myself except for about 30 minutes of help from Brother Baldwin.

This became our home for five years. Here our first child, Lawrence, was born December 3, 1910, and our second child, Lois, March 2, 1913.

There were four or five of our families living in or near Juliaetta who constituted our congregation. I was considered their pastor and preached for them when at home. But in those days there were few settled pastors and no salaried ministers. My income came mostly from meetings that I held. These kept me away from home quite a lot. Rosa went with me some but most of the time she stayed at home with the children. This was hard on both of us but especially on her.

Our income was very meager but we were able to subsist on it and we would not go into debt. We felt it would be better to trust God for one week at a time than to have to trust for past weeks too. When God gave us a pound of butter he expected us to use it before he would give us another pound. However we were careful not to be extravagant. The Lord was good to us and so were the people.

The year 1911 was a busy one. We held an effective meeting up Cottonwood Creek a few miles up from Myrtle, Idaho. Also in the town of Myrtle we won a few disciples. Together these made a nice congregation which was pastored for a few years by Brother Baldwin.

One service stands out vividly in my mind. On Sunday morning I preached on sanctification and in the afternoon on how to get the experience. Among those who came to the altar seeking the experience was a man named Edgar Gibbs. For some reason he had quite a struggle but he felt he must have the experience and would die if he did not get it. After a while he arose and began to speak when the glory of God struck him and be began to shout. As others rejoiced with him the noise spread aboard till people came running to see what was happening. Soon the building was full of people. We began to rejoice, sing and testify right on through the supper hour with no thought of eating. We merged right into the evening service.

At the time for the evening service a few others arrived among them a United Brethren minister who had announced that he would preach that night. But as we were not aware of his intention I preached.

More than forty years later I saw Brother Gibbs and he keenly remembered that experience.

Among others who came from this little group was the Cassell family who did much to help start the church at Clarkston.

In those days we did not wear neckties, Brother Cassell, saw that I wore none so took his off. I wondered how to get Brother Gibbs to take his off as I had no scripture. I decided to let him wait till campmeeting for the brethren to take it off of him.

We had a small group at Reubens where we would preach at times. Not far from there was the town of Melrose. Here we arranged to hold meetings in the Christian church. First we visited the pastor to ask his cooperation. He sought to discourage us saying he would hold a meeting himself but the farmers were too busy to come. But we went ahead with our meeting with fairly good attendance.

One night the pastor came. After the service he attacked me with some fury. He accused me, "Tonight you told the biggest untruth any man ever told in the pulpit." I denied saying what he accused me of and others, including his wife, agreed that I had said no such thing. He said, "Come to hear me Sunday morning and I will answer you." I was not present to hear him but was told he said that such fellows as I should be dead and he would preach my funeral free of charge.

Shortly after that the minister got into a quarrel with one of his members and lost what little religion he had left. That summer he came to the Colfax campmeeting arriving just as the supper bell rang but he would not eat till he found me and asked my forgiveness. He came to the altar, got straightened out, and became one of our pastors.

At Arrow Junction we held services which resulted in the conversion of a young man. After he was baptized he went to Spokane but as he had poor eyesight, and was not familiar with city traffic, he was run over by a car and had his breath knocked out. He was dragged unto the sidewalk and soon a crowd gathered. As soon as he recovered his breath he said, "Praise the Lord." The policeman standing by asked, "What did you say?" If this had happened before he was saved likely the first word would have been an oath. When a kettle boils over it is what is inside that comes out.

About this time Brother Baldwin moved to the town of Southwick, Idaho. Here he became acquainted with several families of good people and sent for me to come and hold a meeting. Our first meeting was held in a lodge hall. This was a profitable meeting in which several families were won to the truth. We held another meeting early in January, 1912. This meeting was held in a chapel furnished by Brother F. M. Helton who partitioned off a part of his carpenter shop for a place of worship. Not only did this man assist in a material way but his godly life was a strong influence. People would say, "If there is a real Christian in this town it is Mr. Helton."

After a few weeks of very profitable services at Southwick we went to Cavendish, near by, where I preached several nights before giving an altar call. After the Sunday morning service a man told me that he and his wife wanted to get saved and wished to know when I would give an invitation. I told him I would do so that night, which I did and both were saved.

Rosa was with me in this meeting and we had our baby with us. One man complained that we dressed the baby too well. As the rains had made the roads very muddy the attendance fell off. This man said, "If John the Baptist were here the mud could not keep the people away." I knew very well I was not John the Baptist.

After this meeting we returned to Southwick and held more services. Since January 1st I had preached 60 times in 60 days. A nice congregation of eight or ten families was established. Brother C. K. Chapman became their pastor and both he and the church where influential and highly respected in the town.

At another time, elsewhere, I preached 57 times in 43 days.

Some interesting things took place at Southwick. One of them concerned Mrs. Frank Thornton.

Sister Thornton was afflicted with erysipelas. We were called to pray for her. After prayer for her healing we sang a song and she sang with us. We told her she might get up when ever she wished to do so. But as soon as we left the room some relatives rushed in and insisted that she stay in bed.

That night, shortly after Brother Baldwin and I had put out the light and gone to bed, we heard someone call, "Mr. Baldwin, Mr. Baldwin; Mrs. Thornton is much worse and wants you to come to pray for her." Immediately we rose and dressed quickly to go to pray for her.

The Thorntons lived perhaps a mile from town. The night was dark and the road was muddy. A few patches of snow could be seen here and there.

As we reached the edge of town we saw white objects of some kind flying past our heads and recognized we were being bombarded. I thought they were snowballs but Brother Baldwin said they were rocks. Suddenely one hit him in the side and he let out a yell that I am sure amused the throwers for it almost amused me too. (I was not hit.) When we arrived at Thornton's we learned they had not sent for us but this was a ruse to get us out on the road. But we were asked to stay the rest of the night, which we did.

The next morning Brother Baldwin, as he picked up his raincoat, asked, "How did I get this grease on my coat?" He put his hand in the pocket and drew out some egg shell. His rock was an egg.

We did not know who attacked us and did not try to find out but our friends were not slow to point the finger at certain church members who did not like our preaching.

Some evangelists arrange a slate of meetings reaching months or even years in advance. This was not my method but usually by the time I closed one meeting I would receive a call for another. I let the Lord arrange my itinerary for me.

About the time the Southwick meeting closed I received a letter from a Mr. Matlock asking me to come to Ahsahka to hold a meeting. This was an Indian village with an Indian church at the mouth of the North Fork of the Clearwater River. A few white people lived there also. I agreed with Mr. Matlock to arrive on a certain day. He said he could not meet the train but would have his children meet me.

On the way to Ahsahka I talked with a man who lived near there and asked him about Mr. Matlock. He replied that he knew every white man in Ahsahka and there was no one by that name; he must be an Indian. So I looked for some papooses to meet me at the train and take me to a shack or possibly a wigwam.

But Mr. Matlock was a white man who had arrived recently from Kentucky. He had learned of me through the Gospel Trumpet. He met me himself and took me to his home.

We held our meeting in the school house with good attendance considering the size of the town. One young man 21 years of age came. He had never been to a church service before.

At the close of the meeting we had baptism in the river. An old timer told me he had lived there 50 years and there had never been a baptism there before.

Here we met an old woman from Kentucky who was the mother of twenty-six children, thirteen of them still living. Although well along in years she seemed strong. She had outlived her husband.

So far as known Brother W. F. Smith was the first church of God man to live in Clarkston. His daughter was to be married and I was asked to perform the ceremony. This was my first experience and I was about as nervous as the bride.

Through Brother Smith's influence Brother T. W. Cooper and I came to Clarkston and held services in the parlor of the Potter Hotel. This was in November, 1912. After a few services we moved across the street to the Vineland Nursery building.

At our first service a Mr. Grimm asked us, "Are you the saints?" We hedged a bit and said "We are not Mormons." Then he asked if we were the people who held campmeeting near Colfax and when we said we were he said, in a loud voice, for he was quite deaf, "Then you are alright." His endorsement helped for he was well known and highly respected in the city. In years to come he was our warm friend A few people were won in these meetings and became permanent members of the church.

In the next three years we had several return engagements at Clarkston including a local assembly. These laid the foundation for the church there. In the summer of 1915 Brother Harry U. Cooper assisted me in a tent meeting at Clarkston which was quite effective.

Brother T. W. Cooper and I held a tent meeting at Nez Perce in 1912 but we had strong competition by the Adventists who were holding a large tent meeting. We had small results except to make a few friends.

On March 2, 1913 our daughter Lois was born. That year I stayed home more. I preached in three or four new places and made visits to a dozen places where I had preached previously. While at home I gave more attention to our small group at Juliaetta. Also I was enabled to be with my family more.

About this time I baptized a Nez Perce Indian young man in the Potlatch Creek near Juliaetta. So far as I know he was the first Nez Perce Indian to come among us. Soon after this Brother Baldwin baptized two or three of their tribe.

One day I received car fare from a lady who wrote, "Come at once and pray for a man with a lingering sickness." I started on the next train. But a cloud burst caused heavy slides covering the tracks in places. I was to change cars at Arrow to go up the River but that line was blocked in several places, so I was taken to Lewiston where I slept (?) on the depot floor. But as the tracks were not yet cleared I returned home and took the first train after service was restored. I went to the closest town then walked the rest of the way.

When I arrived I received a scolding for my delay. I was told a minister should come when sent for if he had to walk all the way. To top it all, the sick man did not want prayer and had not consented to send for me. Needless to say he was not healed.

The year 1914 marked a transition period in my ministry. The Western Washington brethren had purchased a campground at Edmonds and were to have their first campmeeting preceded by a school for ministers for ten days. When the time approached they were short one teacher so sent for me to assist. Ths was a new venture which I will describe more fully later. I preached in the campmeeting also.

Also I ventured far from my usual field by holding a meeting at Sandpoint, Idaho, with Brother T. W. Cooper. We held meeting in a large tent. I preached the first night, which was not unusual, and expected Brother Cooper to share the preaching with me. But he insisted I do all the preaching and he would lead the singing and so it was done that way. Later I helped in a meeting at Addy, Wash., a long way from home.

MY PASTORAL MINISTRY

After ten years of which may be called evangelistic work, with some pastoral service thrown in, my service changed almost wholly to pastoral work, with occasional meetings held at various places.

As I had served in the various meetings held in Clarkston I felt a concern for the work there. We established a Sunday School at the Lincoln school and I had an appointment to preach there every other Sunday. After the tent meeting in 1915, previously mentioned, it was decided that I should move to Clarkston to pastor the church there so we moved from Juliaetta to Clarkston in September, 1915.

The brethren had rented the old Monroe Hotel, the office and parlor to be used for meetings and the back rooms for classes and parsonage. The rent was $10.00 a month which the church paid and also paid the utilities, light and water.

The first Sunday our service consisted of 17 persons, but some of our people were at the Lincoln school Sunday school. Our total membership soon became about fifty.

The growth of the church at Clarkston was due to unforseen causes. I did not know while preaching in the back country that many of our converts would eventually move to Lewiston and Clarkston to use better education facilities. But families of our people came from Pleasant Valley, Stites, Cream Ridge, Myrtle, Nez Perce, and elsewhere. The larger part of the church, in the early days, was made of brethren who had moved in from other places.

Before we had been in Clarkston two years we decided to build a church. We sought a location that would put us some distance from other churches but finally bought right in the midst of the group. The Lewiston-Clarkston Improvement Company, which owned much of the vacant property, offered us a triangular block in the church area. It was their theory that as the business houses were grouped so should the churches be in a group. We were offered this property for $1,400.00 and the Company would donate back $750.00. We bought it and built upon it.

To buy property and build requires money. We secured pledges from members and friends sufficient to give us a good start. All of these pledges were paid in full except one pledge of $5.00. We secured a loan also from our bank.

We did not hire an architect so I drew plans for the church which the trustees approved. Also I made out the principal bill of lumber which we purchased directly from a mill. We had Brother Helton of Southwick as our head carpenter assisted by Brother Holmes, also of Southwick. There was considerable donated labor. I assisted as much as my pastoral duties would permit. Brother Alteneder, of Orofino, donated the plastering.

At the time we were building, the old Methodist church in Lewiston was being torn down. It had many windows of partly colored glass. We bought these windows, including the frames, for $15.00. These furnished nearly all the windows we needed.

The church was dedicated by Brother G. W. Bailey, February 3, 1918. At the same time special meetings were held by Brother S. H. Eddings. This was one of several special meetings held in the next few years. These meetings were fruitful in the salvation of souls and healing of the sick. Brothers S. H. Eddings and O. A. Burgess were especially useful in these meetings. The church was greatly edified and strengthened and remained in a healthy condition during the five years we lived there, 1915 to 1920.

In 1916 we sold our house in Juliaetta and purchased a home at 1108 McCaroll Ave., where we lived the remainder of our time in Clarkston. Here our second daughter, Dorothy, was born November 7, 1919. Brother R. M. Nichols ate supper with us then went to a meeting at the church. When he returned he found that our number had increased with the assistance of Dr. Paul Johnson.

The year 1918 was important to me for this year marked the first time I attended the campmeeting at Anderson. It happened this way: The Inland Empire ministers wished they all might attend but the distance and expense prohibited; so plans were made to send a minister each year who would represent us and speak for us. The previous year Brother S. H. Eddings had been sent and this year it fell my lot to go. I was given credentials to speak for the brethren.

After arriving at Anderson I approached Brother E. A. Reardon, who was chairman of the General Ministerial Assembly, and told him how I had been sent and asked if provision was made to vote by proxy. When he said there was no such provision I asked why not. He replied, "A proxy has no ears."

It was my privilege to attend the first general service in the new tabernacle. Brother D. O. Teasley preached on, "The Manhood of Jesus," text, "Behold the man" (John 19:5). There was a lot of very good preaching. Brother Riggle preached to us ministers a powerful sermon on the subject, "They So Spake," (Acts 14:1).

There seemed to be no fixed program for the meeting. Brethren were appointed to see that the services were properly filled. The morning general services were in charge of G. W. Bailey, the afternoon services in charge of James B. Peterman, and the night services in charge of H. M. Riggle. The preaching was very powerful and inspiring with messages by several ministers.

The Missionary Board, which had been reorganized the previous year, found itself handling funds for home work, such as Missionary Homes, Anderson Bible Training School, Kansas City Bible School and Spokane Bible Institute. The board wished to be freed from this work. A committee was appointed to study these three propositions: (1) One Board to handle foreign affairs only, (2) One Board to handle both home and foreign funds, (3) Two separate Boards. The third suggestion won and two years later the Home Board was formed.

On my way to Anderson I rode on the Great Northern train and stopped off at Grand Forks where the state campmeeting was in progress. The attendance was not large but I met several people who had known my mother and a few that I remembered. As I walked about the streets I looked into the faces of young people trying to recognize them. Then it dawned on me that the young people that I knew sixteen years before were now married and the ones now walking the streets were born since I moved away. But though the people had changed I could still recognize our old home and the schools where I attended. While I was there the pastor, A. G. Ahrendt, conducted the funeral of Jerry Church, a well known doctor who had been wonderfully converted.

I stopped also at Saint Paul Park where I visited the old people's Home and the Scandinavian publishing office. I went on to Chicago and Anderson. I had hoped to see Lake Michigan on the way but if I saw it it was in the form of fog.

At this time the First World War was till in progress but was drawing toward the end. When the Armistice Day arrived, November 11, a great celebration was held in Lewiston-Clarkston. People went wild shouting, "The Kaiser is licked, the Kaiser is licked." One old man rode in a tub behind a car and was thrown out and killed. I spent the day working at the church putting in a cement floor.

The winter of 1918-1919 will be remembered for the great flu epidemic. Many people, sometimes whole families, died. Public meetings such as church services were forbidden. I had the flu, but not bad enough to go to bed. I sat in the house for a week or more with such foolish things as these going through my head:

> "I went to the hencoop on my knees,
> I thought I heard a rooster sneeze;
> He sneezed so hard with the Spanish flu
> He sneezed his gizzard right in two."

And as my breath was very hot:

> "A flu is a device for the escape of hot air.
> My nose is a device for the escape of hot air.
> Therefore I have the flu." (Excuse the logic)

Since public meetings were banned in most cities revivals could not be held so our ministers decided to redeem the time, if possible, by holding a ministers meeting. Portland was suggested for the location but as restrictions were quite severe there it was decided to go to Walla Walla, where the meeting was held in January, 1919. Three important things took place in this meeting:

Brother Oscar Lewis had come prepared to promote his view of tithing as a Christian obligation. As soon as I arrived he began to "buttonhole" me and asked my support to put his view across. I told him I was much interested to hear him after which I should know whether I could support him.

Then Brother Lewis attempted to show that tithing is binding upon all Christians. One of his statements, as I remember it, was "Tithing is an eternal, unalterable law of God written in the moral nature of man." He proceeded from this premise and used three sessions for his discussion. He put over a strong argument and won nearly the entire group of about fifty ministers. He was followed by Brothers G. W. Bailey and E. G. Masters who supported him.

Brother O. A. Burgess, who represented the program committee, asked me what I thought of the presentation. I told him it reminded me of a comment an Advent preacher made concerning a sermon of mine, "It is a very good setting forth from that standpoint." Sensing that I did not agree with Brother Lewis,

Brother Burgess asked me to answer him. I declined to do this as I did not want to cause any strife but, after further urging, I agreed to do so.

When Brother Lewis learned that I would answer him he seemed to direct his arguments to me. He ended his speech with these words, "I have fired a 42 centimeter shell into the camp of the opposition and there is nothing left but the shell hole."

I was given equal time to answer Brother Lewis. I began my speech this way: "Yesterday a 42 centimeter shell exploded in our midst with nothing left but the shell hole. For a time I was not sure that even the hole was left, but when the dust settled, and the smoke cleared away, I found the hole and remembered that many a brave soldier saved his life by taking refuge in a shell hole. So I climbed into the shell hole. I have no cannon, only a rifle. I will name my speech, 'Shots from the shell hole'."

I agreed that giving to God's cause is a moral duty but I denied that this duty is necessarily expressed as a tenth. In the absence of any evidence that Christ ever asked for or received tithes for himself or for his disciples, or than any Christian church practiced tithing the obligation to give a certain fraction of one's income cannot be sustained. I offered no objection to one tithing voluntarily but denied that it is a binding obligation upon all.

I can not make a full statement here but the editor of the Gospel Trumpet had me write my views which he published in late 1921.

By the time I had finished my presentation the entire body of ministers, with one or two exceptions, had come over to my side. But as I had not opposed voluntary tithing a number of the ministers wished to encourage this method. A resolution was adopted and sent to the General Ministerial Assembly asking that we adopt a tithing system.

A second important matter concerned the Spokane Bible Institute. This school had been started several years previously by the church in Spokane and had been taken over by the ministry of the Inland Empire. The proposal was made that the school be taken over by the Northwest Ministerial Assembly, which included the three northwest states. The name of the school was changed to Pacific Bible Institute and a board of trustees were elected consisting of E. G. Masters, C. M. Knight, C. A. Thomas, O. A. Burgess and myself. More about this will be discussed later.

Another matter of some importance was the selection of two ministers to go to Anderson to present our tithing proposal to the General Assembly. E. G. Masters and I were chosen. It was my duty to read the resolution while Brother Masters spoke for it. When he had finished Brother F. G. Smith arose and said, "If tithing is taught in the New Testament it is already our duty to teach and practice it: if it is not there we cannot put it in. " This ended the discussion, though in later years it has been revived.

Brother Burgess had been the teacher at the Spokane Bible Institute and had done an excellent job. But out of his generous spirit he recommended me to be Principal of Pacific Bible Institute. Whether or not he would have accepted the position I do not know but I was chosen. This means I must leave Clarkston when the school would open which was in the fall of 1920.

As I had been sent to Anderson the previous year I thought it a great privilege to be sent again in 1919. Supposing this would be my last trip I arranged to go through Tennessee where I might visit Brother Edgar Gibbs. I went through Salt Lake City, Denver, St. Louis, Hopkinsville, Kentucky and on to Ashland City, Tennessee, where the Gibbs family lived. Here I had a nice visit and experienced true southern hospitality. I preached in the Green Brier church and at the close of the service every man there invited me home with him. Of course I could not go with all of them and it was hard to know which one to choose.

I noticed that when Brother Gibbs would meet anyone on the road he would say, "Youall come go home with us," The reply would be, "No thanks, I caint, youall come home with us." The response would be, "No thanks, we caint this time." I asked Brother Gibbs, "Do you always greet people that way?" He

69

replied, "If you don't they think you are mad at them." I asked, "Do they ever come?" He replied, "Not often, sometimes they do."

Brother Gibbs farmed a bit and raised razor-back hogs. But the acorns were beginning to fall so the hogs might fatten up soon.

After a pleasant visit Brother Gibbs took me to town to get a ride to Nashville. We had to cross the Cumberland River in a row boat. I heard what I thought was an auto horn blow trying to call the ferryman but Brother Gibbs informed me I had heard a bullfrog.

I rode in a car to Nashville and from there took the train to Louisville, Kentucky, and from there on the Big Four to Anderson.

On this trip I passed through eleven states and rode on six different railroads. I visited the Mormon tabernacle in Salt Lake and also looked about Denver. I saw a little of Louisville as well as Nashville. This was not my last trip as I feared it would be but I have not since covered all of the same ground.

Up to the time I moved to Clarkston I had no assured income from any source. When I had been there a short time we began the use of envelopes and adopted a budget. For one or two years the budget provided $500.00 for my support. Our last year, 1919-1920, saw the adoption of a budget of $800.00 for us but the amount that was actually received was $500.00. I made no complaint for we were able to live on this. But Brother George R. Roberts, one of our trustees, said I had been promised $800.00 and he would see that I received it. He gave me his check for $300.00. This money was used in part for my trip to Anderson for the 1920 campmeeting. I thought it advisable that I be there as school matters were likely to be discussed.

The time had come for the creation of a board for home work. "Home Missions" was suggested for the name but the foreign board thought the word "missions" should be reserved for them. The name finally chosen was "Board of Church Extension and Home Missions." A board of nine members was elected and I

70

was one of them. We were brought back the next year, 1921, at which time the Board was incorporated and a new body of members elected. I was dropped off. I had attended four successive campmeetings which I supposed would be all for me.

When we were preparing to leave Clarkston we offered our house for sale. We had shipped our goods to Boise and were preparing to go ourselves on a Monday. On Saturday a man came to see me about chickens he heard I had to sell. When he saw our house empty he asked if it was for rent. I said it would be if we failed to sell. He asked my price which I told him was $4,000. He agreed to buy it if I would throw off the commission, which I did. We closed the deal and two days later were on our way to Boise.

Interest in the church work in Southern Idaho centered about Pacific Bible Institute but the general work of the church was not neglected. There were a few small congregations which were cared for principally by Brothers W. W. Crist and E. G. Masters. Each year a campmeeting was held at Middleton. But in the year 1921 the meeting was held in a park at Boise. This was a very good meeting. One special feature was the presence of Brother H. C. Kramer from Kenya Colony in Africa. He had come to the United States to arrange for the transfer of the mission work in Nyanza Province to our Mission Board. This has become our most fruitful mission.

We had regular church services in Boise attended by the students and a few others. Church work was conducted also at Middleton, Deer Flat, Twin Falls, and a few other places.

Upon our arrival in Boise I bought our first car which was an Overland, Model 4. I could drive it 25 miles per gallon, per hour. I bought a bicycle for Lawrence also. Our youngest child, Harold, was born November 10, 1921.

Since the ministers had decided to move the school to Seattle we made preparations to move there. We shipped our goods and loaded our car and drove to Edmonds where we attended the

71

campmeeting and later moved into Seattle. I preached a few times at Edmonds.

The school was closed at the end of the first semester. I was paid my January salary and released in the dead of winter. In the next two months I held four meetings at places where I was invited. I preached 64 times and 45 people received spiritual experiences. I returned home for my birthday, March 18.

Soon after this I preached at Kennewick and assisted Brother Nichols in a meeting at Pasco in the Old Methodist church. At the close of the meeting we organized a Sunday School with a membership of 25 people.

Shortly after this Brother Nichols resigned as pastor at Walla Walla and I was asked to succeed him. So we began to make preparations to move to Walla Walla. On May 15 we started in our Overland on our way to Walla Walla. This was the first day that Snoqualamie Pass was open and we found the snow six feet deep. But the next day, as we passed through Kennewick we saw people picking strawberries.

When we arrived in Walla Walla we found a revival in progress with Brother Eddings as the evangelist. I was asked to conduct the singing. One night, much to my surprise, a group of men, robed and hooded, marched in during the service and presented the church with an American flag. They left without a word.

Shortly after the close of this meeting Brother Nichols moved to Colfax and I took over the pastorate at Walla Walla and purchased Brother Nichol's house where we lived while in Walla Walla.

Not too long after I moved to Walla Walla the church at Milton, Oregon, about thirteen miles away, was without a pastor. For a while I pastored both churches. While Sunday school was in progress at Walla Walla I would preach at Milton, then hurry back to Walla Walla in time to preach there. About this time I held a revival at Milton in which ten were converted. Also, for a time, I conducted a midweek service at Burbank.

72

While we were living in Walla Walla our church was visited by Brother J. W. Phelps, Secretary of the Missionary Board, and Brother George Olson, missionary to Jamaica. Also it was my privilege to hear G. Campbell Morgan and H. A. Ironsides. It was during this time that I wrote my book, The Menace of Mormonism, which was published in 1926. I have been told that many Mormons have been lead out through reading this book.

Early in 1924 I attended the Northwest Ministerial Assembly at Spokane. This meeting was disturbed somewhat by contact with Pentecostalism. Brothers C. G. Myers and Guy DeFreese had become entangled with this movement and withdrew from us taking with them their congregations and the church buildings at Centralia and Olympia. These buildings were recovered later at considerable cost but the men never returned. The church at Wenatchee was lost to us also through "fifth column" methods. The name on the building, "Church of God," was enlarged to read, "Pentecostal Church of God Four Square." None of the churches in the Inland Empire were lost though some of the people were led astray.

A short time later I held a meeting for my brother George at the Dean and Ash Streets Church of God. This was a successful and profitable meeting, one of the best held in Spokane in years.

While living in Walla Walla we experienced somewhat of a recession which affected church finance. Part of the time I found work to add to our income. But as I preferred to preach rather than anything else I accepted a few calls for meetings. I preached at Craigmont and Post Falls and attended the Young People's Convention at Sandpoint. Also I made a brief trip to Stites. While there a rock slide closed the tunnel at Orofino cutting off train service beyond that point. As there was no other means of travel I walked from Stites to Orofino as I had done nineteen years before.

This year I was called to Canada to be the evangelist at the Saskatchewan campmeeting at Saskatoon and the Alberta campmeeting at Provost.

I learned through the Gospel Trumpet that I had been elected to the Missionary Board. I remained a member for thirty-five years.

Early in 1925 I conducted a meeting at Rainier, Oregon, where Brother C. K. Chapman was pastor. While I was there I preached also at the Staymen school house, not far from Rainier.

At that time the Yakima church was without a pastor. I was asked to help them out so went over a few times to preach for them. I attended the Anderson campmeeting in June and had my introduction to the Missionary Board. The work of missions seemed very complicated to me, and such it was and is. I preached at the campmeeting on The Kinkdom of God. On my return I attended the Colfax campmeeting and later the Edmonds campmeeting. Shortly after the Colfax campmeeting I resigned at Walla Walla and moved to Yakima. At Yakima I was busy in regular pastoral work and also at the request of the Gospel Trumpet Company I wrote a series of doctrinal Sunday School lessons.

Again in 1926 I attended the Anderson campmeeting returning through Canada on the Canadian National Railway and by boat from Vancouver to Seattle. This was a very pleasant trip.

While at Anderson a friend asked me if I could be available to come to Park Place church. As the suggestion was not at all official I thought little of it. But shortly after I received an official letter asking me to consider coming to Park Place. For sometime I had felt that I would go to Anderson but I never supposed it would be in that capacity. Although I considered it a great responsibility I agreed to go and offered my resignation to the church at Yakima.

After attending the Edmonds campmeeting we started our trip to Anderson. We traded our Overland in on a Dodge car and drove first to Paradise Park at Mt. Mainier, then to Seaside, Oregon, to see the Pacific before leaving, then to Walla Walla, then Troy and Deary, Idaho, on through Yellowstone Park, North and South Dakota, and on to Indiana arriving there on August thirty-first. That same night I conducted a wedding service without even time to dress up.

ANDERSON, INDIANA — 1927

The seven years spent in Anderson, 1926-1933, were, in some respects, the most profitable years of my life. Here I came to know the leaders of the movement and to work with them. I suppose I gave some contribution to the work but I think I received much more than I gave. Our congregation included officers and employes of the Gospel Trumpet Company, Anderson College, and other boards with many students and teachers as well as a large number of just common people. Among our number were twenty or more ministers. These formed an unofficial council of elders who gave me valuable advice and assistance.

In my opinion my preaching was the strongest feature of my ministry with my pastoral work next. I think my administration was my weakest service for I was not so much a leader as a companion of the flock. I was well aware that among the flock were stronger leaders than I was and I leaned on them for counsel.

Shortly before leaving for Anderson my book of sermon outlines was stolen so I arrived in Anderson without my best outlines. I thought this would be a handicap but really it was a blessing for I was required to construct new sermons and these reflected the new circumstances and surroundings which I now faced. Of course I made considerable use of the ministers in the congregation.

A few months after my arrival we planned a revival meeting. Whom to secure for the evangelist was a question. Brother J. W. Lykins and another minister were suggested. It was the opinion of our ministers that the other minister was the better speaker but that Brother Lykins would get more people saved. We decided on Brother Lykins who came and we had a successful revival.

We had other very successful revivals. One of these was held by Brother Riggle which was very largely attended. One night I counted forty ministers present.

75

We had one protracted meeting which could not be called a success. It was rather a detriment. A certain evangelist had a meeting announced to begin in two weeks for a congregation in another city. We arranged for him to hold a meeting for us during the weeks that intervened. He took over full control so that I never felt less needed or more in the way. He assumed a super-spiritual attitude and preached every night, except one (and that one was a flop), from the second chapter of Acts. He urged all who would like to be more spiritual to come to the altar, many came. He would say, "We are not classifying you, just come and be blessed." Those who came did not know what they needed or wanted and did not know what, if anything, they had received. Many became confused as to their spiritual state and considerable division resulted.

When the two weeks were up the evangelist postposed his other meeting that he might remain with us another week. At the end of the third week he wanted to stay longer. But as I could see the harm that was coming to the church I took the bit in my teeth and announced, "The meeting will close tonight."

Later this evangelist worked his way into another of our churches in Anderson and soon had it badly divided. He left the church and drew away some members after him. This evangelist told me that God had raised up D. S. Warner but now a new era has come and God is raising up another leader. He did not say that he was the man but his attitude plainly revealed his ambition to be that person.

I opened our pulpit to another man who was supposed to be one of our ministers. He took the opportunity to deride the movement and our early leaders and to exalt himself. I felt like stopping him but I considered the source, like the man who was kicked by a mule, knowing that before long he would "hang himself."

Before I had been in Anderson a year I was elected president of the Missionary Board. This was a great responsibility for me with so little knowledge about the many problems connected with this position. But I gave earnest attention to the work so that one member of the board told me that I was the best president the board ever had. I doubt that I deserved this compliment, but I did my best. I served in this position for six years, so long as I remained in Anderson.

. As president of the Missionary Board it became my privilege to attend meetings of the Foreign Missionary Conference of North America which were held, usually, at Atlantic City, New Jersey. Here I heard such Christian leaders as John R. Mott, Robert E. Speer, and others.

Also I represented our movement on the Near East Relief Committee of which Henry Morganthau Sr. was chairman. It was at a promotion dinner in New York that Mr. Morganthau challenged us with this story: "A baby was left in a basket on a porch. The man of the house found it and brought it into the house; but the family decided they could not be bothered with the baby so he put it back on the porch where it froze to death. If he had not taken the baby in but had notified the police he would have been clear; but for putting the baby out again he was held guilty of murder. We have taken on the care of Near East refugees: we dare not put them back on the porch." A budget of $6,000,000 was adopted; I am not sure that it was raised. I was appointed also on the Committee of China Relief but rendered no particular service.

On my trips to the east coast I was privileged to stop at Philadelphia and Washington as well as at New York, Baltimore and Niagara Falls. It was my privilege to shake hands with President Calvin Coolidge. Earlier I had seen Presidents Theodore Roosevelt and William Howard Taft.

When I feel a little inclined to brag I tell that I ate with President Hoover. I did not eat out of the same plate with him nor was I in the same room, or under the same roof, but we were in the same city. Also at one time I lived in the White House— all of seventeen minutes, as a tourist. Also I sat in the senate chamber but did not join in the discussion. Once I spoke in the

Mormon Tabernacle, at Salt Lake—to the man sitting next to me.

When I moved to Anderson in 1926 I was already a trustee of Anderson College. Before long I was placed on the Executive Committee of the College and served one term as Vice-President. I taught for Brother Morrison his class in homiletics for a brief period. In the year 1929-1930 I taught Old Testament Introduction and New Testament Introduction. These classes had been taught by Russel Byrum but because of criticism against him he retired from the faculty.

My teaching load took some of my time. To compensate for this one of the College professors, Brother Sherwood, agreed to do pastoral visiting for me in exchange for my teaching service.

Although no longer a member of the Board of Church Extension and Home Missions I served for a time on its Executive Committee.

Shortly after coming to Anderson I gave my first radio address over station WHBU. We broadcast over this station our Sunday morning service for three years. On several occasions I broadcast over WOWO, Fort Wayne, for the Board of Church Extension. This was a forerunner of the Christian Brotherhood Hour, which was established later by this Board. Since then I have spoken over several stations in various cities, sometimes a single service, and sometimes a series of sermons. Most of these were live but some were transcriptions.

While I lived in Anderson there were six congregations of the Church of God in the city, all working harmoniously together. The Park Place church was by far the largest and it furnished the others with leaders and financial assistance when needed. Our influence in the city was great. Also we found a high type of Protestant ministers with whom it was easy to cooperate in matters of common interest.

But the depression, which came suddenly and lasted several years, brought us difficulties. We had considered building an educational unit but were forced to defer this. Many of our people were out of work and I counted as many as 300 of our people who moved away because of the depression. Nevertheless we survived. My salary was reduced and when the church was ashamed to reduce it further I accepted the budgeted amount then returned $25.00 a month besides my regular giving; but we survived, and so did the church.

After I had been in Anderson more than six years I began to feel that I should resign before long, so I announced to the church that I would resign the following spring. This was to give them plenty of time to secure my successor. Brother Reardon, the former pastor, had gone to Denver largely for the health of his son Willard and was not willing to return.

For some time I had felt a desire to return to the West Coast but had no place in sight. I had been approached concerning coming to Portland but was not ready yet to leave. I felt a desire to go to Seattle but so far as I knew they were not contemplating a change. But shortly before my resignation at Anderson became effective I received a letter from Seattle stating that Brother Schlatter was leaving and asking if I would consider coming to them. I felt this was of the Lord so agreed to come. It was our plan to move to Seattle after the Anderson campmeeting, which we did.

In June of 1933 I completed my second term as president of the Missionary Board and as I had already resigned as pastor of the Park Place church and had agreed to go to Seattle as pastor of the Woodland Park Avenue church I felt that I could not accept another term as president of the Board. It is necessary that the president live at or near Anderson. At the same time Brother Riggle declined renomination as secretary which is the executive office and is salaried.

The Board appointed a nominating committee consisting of F. G. Smith, C. E. Byers and E. A. Reardon. This committee approached me about being nominated for secretary. I told them I had agreed to go to Seattle. But the committee, particularly Brothers Smith and Byers, urged me to consent to run saying I was needed and Seattle could get someone else. Reluctantly I consented to run.

Brother Adam Miller, who had been a missionary in Japan, was nominated also. I hoped he would be elected, and he was. He proved to be an excellent secretary and later president whereas I was happy in my work in Seattle. I believe God had his way.

After I had announced my intention to resign Brother Reardon was invited to return to Park Place which invitation he accepted. He arrived in Anderson shortly before the campmeeting. On the last Sunday before the campmeeting (there are no services during campmeeting) I preached my farewell sermon in the morning service and Brother Reardon gave the baccalaureate sermon for the graduates of Anderson College in the evening.

The church served a "breakfast dinner" after the morning service. This served as a farewell to me and my family and also a welcome to Brother Reardon and his family.

After shipping our goods we entered our car and started for Seattle on July 1 after living in Anderson seven years lacking two months. My wife Rosa, Lois, Dorothy and Harold were with me. Lawrence remained in Anderson where he had a good job with the Bulletin and eventually worked up to the position of printer. We hoped he would come west later but he remained in Anderson till his death. He was mortally wounded in a car accident in 1943.

We passed through Chicago and visited the World's Fair, then on westward to Wyoming where we visited Yellowstone Park, then on and on to Seattle. One day we broke an axle which delayed us nearly a whole day but we reached Seattle July 11, as we had planned.

We were furnished the parsonage in which to live and as it was heated from the same tank as was the church our heat was furnished. Otherwise we paid our own utilities and lived on our salary of $20.00 a week which, in time, grew to $100.00 a month.

The day we arrived in Seattle I went with one of the brethren to Edmonds where we had a cottage prayermeeting. In earlier years there had been a good church at Edmonds but now the few Edmonds families were considered members of the Woodland Park church. I established a preaching appointment there, first in the Library building, then in the Coterie club, where we established a Sunday school. I secured Brother Byrum Martin to assist me and he soon became pastor and built up a nice congregation.

We found the Woodland Park church in Seattle in good spiritual condition for Brother Schlatter had done a good work. During the five years we were in Seattle we made some progress and people were added to the church.

It was during the pastorate of Brother S. S. Johnson that the brick Woodland Park church was constructed. The ground floor was completed but the auditorium was left unfinished. Efforts were made to raise money with which to finish it but before enough money could be raised it was needed and used for other purposes. At one time, soon after my arrival, payments on the mortgage were so difficult to meet that it was suggested we turn the property over to the mortgagee, but he refused to accept it and reduced our payments.

We found it difficult to raise money with which to finish the auditorium for fear it would be used for other purposes, so we adopted the policy that any money contributed would be spent at once for lath and volunteer labor would nail it on. Through this method in time the whole room was lathed. Then we raised enough money to buy the plaster and Brothers Earl and Howard Timmons and Arthur Buckbee from Portland came and did the plastering without charge. The only one hired was a man to mix the plaster. A goodly number of brethren in the church, including myself, gave hours of labor to finish the job.

Of course all of these brethren knew me except the man who mixed the plaster. He, seeing me dressed in work clothes, supposed I was there to wait on him. He would order me to bring him sacks of plaster and buckets of sand which I would do. One day I was called to conduct a funeral. When he saw me dressed in my Prince Albert coat and derby he was surprised and embarrassed. I thought it a good joke.

We moved the seats up from the lower floor and the ladies bought some strips of carpet for the aisles. Soon we were using and enjoying our completed sanctuary. We continued to use the lower floor for Sunday School classes and also for baptisms as it contained the baptistry. It was available also for other purposes.

My pastorate at Seattle continued from 1933 to 1938 when I was succeeded by Brother M. J. Hooker. These were happy years in which the church made normal progress. Besides caring for our local church I preached occasionally for others. I preached some at Auburn and Tekoa and at various conventions as well as giving addresses over the radio. There were occasional baptisms, marriages and funerals. On February 27, 1935 I married our daughter Lois to John Linsey Grover of Edmonds. Soon after their marriage they moved to Wrangell, Alaska, where they lived for several years. A year later we became grandparents.

These were years of depression so money was not very plentiful. We were furnished the parsonage and were able to get along. We had our two younger children, Dorothy and Harold, in school.

When plans were made for establishing Pacific Bible College, about which more will be said later, it became evident that I would be associated with the school. I was chosen as one of the trustees who became the incorporators. Also I was elected president. This meant I must resign as pastor at Seattle. I continued to serve both during the first school year.

My association with the Seattle church was very cordial and I disliked to leave but I felt called of the Lord and the church to this other position. I accepted without obligation. I have never felt regret over the change as I have found this service equally rewarding.

The following pages will tell more about the College and about ministerial education in general among us.

I should say also that my wife, Rosa, was very active in women's work of the church. She organized the Washington Women's Missionary Society in 1933 and was the first president of the society, the first in the Pacific Northwest.

MINISTERIAL TRAINING IN THE CHURCH OF GOD
Particularly in the Pacific Northwest

It is well known that not many of our early ministers were highly educated. Few if any of them were college graduates. But they were diligent students of the Bible with the aid of marginal references, Cruden's concordance, and available good books. One who knew them well could scarcely doubt that they were assisted by the Holy Spirit. In their self education they compared well with such pioneer preachers as the Methodist circuit riders.

It would be wrong to suppose that these men were opposed to education though no one valued it as highly as we do today. When I was a boy I heard a young minister express a desire to attend a seminary but he knew of none that taught the central truths of our message, but rather each seminary taught its own peculiar brand of theology. He could find no suitable place to go. Our ministers were inclined to brand seminaries hot beds of heresy, and they were not far wrong. It is no wonder that they called D.D.'s "dumb dogs."

The young man who felt called to the ministry found his best opportunity for training in accompanying an older minister. These older ministers were nearly all "flying evangelists" who held protracted meetings. The young men who accompanied them were soon well trained in the message and methods of the ministry. This method was apostolic.

Early in the Twentieth Century there sprang up a number of Missionary Homes. These were located in New York, Chicago, Kansas City, Denver, Oakland, Portland, Spokane, Seattle, and other cities. The Spokane Home was built in 1904. The following year George W. Bailey returned from India and became pastor of the church in Spokane and occupied the Home. A number of young men and women were soon living in the Home and engaging in spiritual work.

These Missionary Homes were training schools for young workers who were given practical experience in visitation work and the distribution of literature including the lending libarary work. Also they taught Sunday School classes and held prayer-meetings.

Each winter, for several years, a school of Bible instruction was conducted in Spokane. Brother Bailey, the pastor, conducted classes in Bible Geography, Bible History, Music Theory and Sight Singing, and related subjects, for the benefit of the local workers.

In the year 1907 O. A. Burgess, with his young family came to Spokane from Kansas. He was converted in the Spokane camp-meeting that year and soon entered the ministry. His education was much above that of the rest of us. He soon became an efficient minister and teacher. It was only natural that Brother Bailey should use him in this teaching work.

The interest of Brother Burgess soon reached beyond Spokane so he arranged a reading course for ministers which he conducted on a correspondence plan. He gave assignments and occasional examinations. The first course was given in 1915 and included such subjects as: The Old Testament, How We Got Our Bible, Between the Testaments, Philosophy of the Plan of Salvation, The Pastor, Ancient History. The course was arranged in six periods of six weeks each and the student was asked to read in a separate book each day of the week (six days). Thus he could avoid cramming at the end of a period.

It was my privilege to take some of this work which I found to be very helpful. I also took some work with Bible Study by Mail which was a correspondence course conducted by the New York Home under the direction of D. O. Teasley with courses prepared by A. D. Kahn and G. P. Tasker and others. This too was very helpful.

The efforts of Brother Burgess in behalf of ministerial training aroused so much interest that it was decided to open a day school in Spokane and to welcome all who could come. The announcement listed these subjects: Studies in the Old Testament, Ancient History, Bible Geography, Bible Manners and Customs, Elementary English, and music. Also there would be lectures by Brother Bailey on The Work of the Ministry and Homiletics.

Each student was required to do an amount of spiritual work such as visiting and literature distribution and "to take an active part in services on Sunday."

Expenses were at the minimum: tuition $3.00 a month, board $3.25 a week. Board and room near church $5 to $6 a week. If one could bring his own bedding he might room free in the church attic.

With the aid of donated materials and voluntary labor a small school building was erected on the church property. Invitations were sent out and students came from as far as 200 miles away. Among those who attended and later became well known were R. M. Nichols, Ira J. Masters, C. C. Miller, Alva Rieckers and George Fickel.

The school opened October 2, 1916, under the name of "Spokane Bible School of the Church of God. G. W. Bailey, Supt. O. A. Burgess Teacher in charge." Soon the school became sponsored by the ministers of the Inland Empire and was called Spokane Bible Institute. It was one of the three schools recognized by the ministry at Anderson.

At the Northwest Ministerial Assembly held at Walla Walla in January, 1919, the control of the school was transferred from the brethren of the Inland Empire to the Northwest Ministerial Assembly and was renamed Pacific Bible Institute. Plans were instituted for the reorganization and relocation of this school. Thus ends one glorious chapter in its existance.

A New Era In The Northwest

The development of ministerial education in the Northwest was due, in a measure, to the coming of Brother E. G. Masters among us. He came to Spokane from Minneapolis in about 1910. He was a dynamic preacher and a good leader. He was especially helpful for the young ministers. Up to this time the younger ministers were little more than carbon copies of the older ministers. No young man would venture to declare anything he had not heard an older minister say. The pattern was set by the older ministers, in the Inland Empire particularly by Brother Bailey. Brother Masters encourage us younger men to do some independent thinking for ourselves, not in a critical or independent spirit but for wholesome development of our intellect. The effect was quite stimulating and helpful.

The brethren in Western Washington purchased a campground at Edmonds. The first campmeeting on these grounds was held in 1914. At that time Brother Masters was living in Seattle. Under his leadership a ten days gospel workers institute was held preceeding the campmeeting. The persons chosen to lead the institute were E. G. Masters, G. W. Bailey, O. A. Burgess and James R. Tallen. For some reason Brother Tallen was unable to serve so I was called at the last minute to take his place.

The courses outlined covered a variety of subjects and naturally could not be thorough for lack of time. Brother Masters taught The Ministry, Psychology, Phrenology, Homiletics, and gave lectures on Revelation. Brother Bailey taught Foreign Missions and Music Theory. Brother Burgess taught Bible Analysis, Bible History, Bible Geography and Pastoral Ministry. I taught English Grammar and speech, also Logic and Parliamentary Law. We had 18 students the first year.

A similar institute was held at Edmonds in connection with the 1915 campmeeting with the same leaders in charge. This also was a very successful effort. The following year, 1916, something similar was conducted in connection with the Colfax campmeeting. Brother Masters was not present. Brother Bailey was in general charge though Brother Burgess and I did most of the teaching. We decided that in the following year, 1917, we would have two institutes, one in Spokane to be conducted by Brother Burgess and one at Clarkston which I would conduct. On account of the war Brother Burgess cancelled his but I went through with mine though the students were mostly girls with a few older men.

Although this institute plan was not perpetuated it did much to encourage ministerial training which later found its place in the Bible Institutes.

Pacific Bible Institute

As previously stated control of the Spokane Bible Institute was transferred from the ministers of the Inland Empire to the Northwest Ministerial Assembly in 1919. A rather loose organization consisting of ministers and laymen was formed to make plans for the new school. However the main responsibility fell into the hands of the Board of Trustees which consisted of five members, namely, E. G. Masters, O. A. Burgess, C. A. Thomas, C. M. Knight and A. F. Gray. The Board was organized with A. F. Gray, President, C. M. Knight, Vice-president, C. A. Thomas, Secretary, O. A. Burgess, Treasurer and E. G. Masters, Financial Field Secretary, whose job was to secure "scholars and dollars." This Board was charged also with securing a location for the school. The church in Spokane offered us the Missionary Home for $40.00 a month rent. This seemed very reasonable but some of the brethren thought it desirable to move to a new place.

It now became the duty of the Board to find a new place for the school. Properties were inspected at Walla Walla and Yakima in Washington and at Baker and Woodburn in Oregon and at Nampa in Idaho. While at Woodburn we concluded that we would need about $100,000.00 to do all we wanted to do. Somehow the information leaked out and out came a newspaper report: "The Church of God has decided to establish a university in Woodburn and will invest in property here to the amount of $100,000.00."

At that time Brother Masters lived in Boise and was very eager to have the school located there. Through the use of statistics and maps he proved (?) that Boise, being in the center of everything, was the ideal place for the school. (It is true that Boise is at the center of the earth's surface; one might fly 25,000 miles staight ahead and find himself right back at Boise!) With his persuasion he won the day and Boise was chosen as the place for the school.

Brother Masters found a mansion-like house with beautiful surroundings which we all thought would make an ideal home for the school. It was for sale at about $50,000. Although the money was not in sight we offered to buy it with a down payment of $1,000. The lady who owned it agreed but her husband refused to sell with so small a down payment. Failing in this we purchased for $8,000 at 1311 Bannock Street with a small house in the rear. This served to house the students.

The Boise school system had abandoned their Hawthorne school. Brother Masters succeeded in securing the use of the building for one year free of charge. This gave us ample class rooms. For the second year we rented a hall down town where we held classes and also held church services for the first semester. To save rent we arranged to have classes in the dormitory the second semester.

Classes began at Pacific Bible Institute October 5, 1920, with ten students enrolled. Before the end of the second year we reached the total of nineteen students. These students came from California, Oregon, Washington and Idaho. I served as principal of the school and was assisted by Brother O. A. Roush, a public school teacher and minister, from Visalia, California. Our curriculum covered a wide area of subjects, included were these:

Grammar	Introductory Bible	Exegesis
History	Pastoral Theology	Typology
Logic	Spelling	Religious Education
Hermeneutics	Church History	Biblical Analysis
Bible History	Psychology	Music
Theology		

Naturally it would be difficult to cover all these subjects in a two years course in a thorough manner. Nevertheless a lot of material was studied and much information was imparted.

When the Northwest Ministerial Assembly met at Woodburn in December, 1920, with several California brethren present, a more complete organization for the Institute was devised. The existing board of trustees was retained and a Board of Overseers was set up. This Board was composed of, J. W. Byers, L. W. Guilford, H. A. Schlatter, W. H. DeWhitt and W. A. Warner, of California; E. J. Axup, G. T. Neal and J. J. Gillespie, of Oregon; S. H. Eddings, R. M. Nichols and Ira J. Masters, of the Inland Empire; C. A. Thomas, E. H. Ahrendt and Oscar Lewis, of Western Washington; and E. G. Masters, C. M. Knight and C. K. Chapman, of Idaho. This Board had its own chairman and secretary and three committees—one on curriculum, one on finance and one on location. The brethren were not sure that Boise was the best location for the Institute. Some months later the decision was made to move the school to Seattle.

Although the attendance at Boise was lower than we had expected it to be we did not feel that the effort was in vain. Of all nineteen one has gone to Pentecostalism, one became a Methodist minister, but so far as I know all the others remained true to the church. Among those who became somewhat well known are C. H. Beahm, P. H. Berg, Mary (Jarvis) West and Grace (Chase) Kole.

The decision had been made to move the school to Seattle after the close of the second school year. When the time came to move we loaded our family of six in our Baby Overland and piled in it and on it all it could hold. We headed for the Edmonds campmeeting which was about to begin. We left Boise Monday morning and that day we reached Baker. Our load was very heavy for a light car and the sun was hot so we had lots of tire trouble. The second we reached The Dalles. Here we bought a new tire and stayed over night. On Wednesday we reached Portland and Thursday night we camped near Centralia. As we traveled northward the next day we were greeted with cool breezes from Puget Sound and made our way to Seattle and Edmonds Friday afternoon.

We had given some thought to locating the school on the campground so we might use the facilities there. But this did not seem feasable as no employment for students was available. So we settled in Seattle and were given a large room in the Woodland Park church, then located on Whitman Avenue, near the present church, to be used as a class room. Students could find homes with the church families.

In the meantime Brother Masters had moved to Oklahoma so very little promoting was done. The enrollment was again disappointing. We had good evening classes of local people but our day classes were small. We had one student from Canada, Brother Harry Gardner, who later became president of Alberta Bible Institute.

The Northwest Ministerial Assembly was held in Seattle at the Christmas season 1922-1923. The matter of the Institute received much attention. There was no dissatisfaction as to the curriculum or finances but there was disappointment concerning the enrollment. Possibly this could have been overcome and remedied by more earnest promotion. But instead the ministers decided to close the school, temporarily, hoping that a greater interest might soon arise. No one supposed the period of waiting would cover fourteen years.

In the year 1930, while I lived in Anderson, I made a trip to the West with some other brethren. While I was in the West I learned that there was a desire to have the school reopened. I was approached about the matter, but no one seemed to know just how to go about it so the matter was laid to rest for a few more years.

The General School Situation

It seems best at this point to consider the school situation as it was viewed by the brethren at Anderson. There was considerable discussion of the subject at the campmeeting of 1918. The Anderson Bible Training School had opened the previous fall as a division of the Gospel Trumpet Company work. The school was intended to be helpful in part, though not exclusively, for the employes of the Gospel Trumpet Company. Spokane Bible Institute had been in operation for a few years and the Kansas City Bible School had been in operation perhaps longer. At any rate these three schools were operating in 1918.

There was considerable discussion in which F. G. Smith, L. H. Morgan, J. T. Wilson, J. C. Blaney, and others took part. All of these expressed the need of education for our young ministers and yet they felt the need of great caution. A majority of the colleges east of the Mississippi were started by churches but most of them eventually got out of hand.

The Assembly appointed a committee to give consideration to the school question. This committee consisted of D. O. Teasley, J. W. Phelps, R. L. Berry, A. F. Gray and R. H. Owens. Our discussion concerned chiefly the scope and relation of the three schools. I suppose I was chosen because of my knowledge of the Spokane school and Brother Berry, of Missouri, because of his relation to the Kansas City school.

The position was taken and conceded, that any work of a general nature was entitled to general support. As the Spokane school was so far away it would be expected to draw students and support from its own territory. The Kansas City school was expected, so someone thought, to draw its students and support chiefly from Missouri, whereas the Anderson school would serve the church in general and be entitled to general support.

Brother Berry opposed this conclusion vigorously. He declared the Kansas City school benefitted the whole church and if it was not entitled to general support neither was Anderson. He said that Missouri could support the Kansas City school by itself, if need be, but this would lessen its giving to other causes.

Our committee made no formal report, as I can recall, but the

Assembly adopted the following resolution, reported in the Gospel Trumpet of July 4, 1918.

"The ministerial assembly also decided that there should be created a general Educational Fund to be held by the Missionary Board of the church of God, and that this fund should be distributed to the existing Bible training-schools in proportion to the number of enrolled students . . . We trust many . . . will gladly contribute to the Educational Fund so that our young ministers and gospel workers may be able to secure such elementary training as these schools provide . . ."

The Assembly appointed another committee consisting of F. G. Smith, H. M. Riggle and J. C. Blaney to bring in a resolution dealing with Anderson Bible Training School. Their report follows.

(Quoting in part from the same issue of the G.T.)

"There is a human side to every minister's qualification and work; that he must have some general knowledge and information derived from careful and prayerful sutdy; that the question of training-schools is merely a question of method, since all God-ordained ministers feel the need of securing, in some manner, all the education that they can use to the glory of God." The ministerial body decided in favor of such a school, with the following restrictions:

"1. We believe that such a school can be conducted to the glory of God and the welfare of the ministry and church if kept within certain bounds.

"2. We believe that no effort should be made to create a sentiment to the effect that young ministers must attend this school in order to secure recognition.

"3. It is our opinion that in many cases the education of ministers can best be obtained in the sections of the country where their ministerial work is to be done . . . In other words, we do not believe that the Anderson Bible Training-School should supercede or replace other training-schools of the church.

"4. Students should be left free to choose their own course of study from among such branches as the school provides.

"5. No recommendation or diploma should be given to any student. (This statment is elaborated at length.)

"6. We believe that the training of ministers in this school should include more than their intellectual development along educational lines. The most prominent feature must be their personal development in spirituality, faith, and gifts of the Spirit of God."

The Assembly adopted this resolution though there followed considerable agitation concerning the granting of diplomas. The matter was referred again to a committee for further study. It may have been the same committee for Brother Riggle was on it. He gave the committee's report which was, "We recommend that without further discussion a ballot be taken as to whether Anderson Bible Training School may issue diplomas to its students." There were 180 ballots cast, 74 yes, 106 no. This decision was reversed in a few years and the Anderson school now gives diplomas and confers degrees.

It is noticable that though both Brother Riggle and Brother Smith were hesitant about giving diplomas they were the first two on whom Anderson conferred the degree of Doctor of Divinity. Both of these brethren had preached against "dumb dogs" as many others have, but one may change his mind if he sees he is wrong.

It seems desirable to relate more matters concerning Anderson Bible Training School before returning to the West. Brother J. T. Wilson, as president of the Gospel Trumpet Company, was instrumental in getting the school started and was its principal for six years before he moved from Anderson. In 1919 he secured Brother John A. Morrison to become his assistant and who succeeded Wilson as principal, then later became president. If my source of information is correct Otto F. Linn served as principal of the Kansas City Bible School as early as 1918. O. A. Burgess filled this position also not much later.

As early as 1918 the suggestion was made that Kansas City join with Anderson. When and why the Kansas City School closed I do not know but for a number of years with Pacific Bible Institute closed also, the whole field was left to Anderson College.

After a few years of operation as a department of the Gospel Trumpet Company, which also conducted an Old People's Home and other projects, it was planned that the college should become a separate institution. A new corporation was formed in 1925 and a board of trustees elected including myself as a member. I remained on the board 21 years and was its chairman 14 years and as well served on the Executive Committee for some time. About half of this time I was also president of Pacific Bible College—carrying water on both shoulders—but I didn't spill very much. The Gospel Trumpet Company deeded its Home with four acres to the College with the approval of the Assembly.

The college continued to grow but it had its difficulties. Some students carried stories to ministers which created some misgivings concerning the teachings of R. R. Byrum. Such stories grow fast and large. The Curriculum Committee might have examined the matter but the administration invited a larger group of ministers to judge in the matter. Feelings had become quite tense.

The large group of ministers met at the Park Place church to hear the matter. After much discussion and explanations the group decided that there was no evidence of heretical teaching and they cleared Brother Byrum while saying that if the charges had been proved true they should have condemned him. Feelings were very strong and some ministers thought the matter had been whitewashed. One minister was so beside himself that referring to a tree behind the Old Auditorium he declared, "Byrum should be hanged on that tree!"

Although Byrum had been cleared the tension was so strong that he thought he should resign from the college faculty, which he did. The trustees refused to accept his resignation till they became convinced he would not remain.

The situation left the college without its teacher of Bible. Brother Earl Martin was secured to teach Systematic Theology and as previously mentioned, I was chosen to teach Old Testament Introduction and New Testament Introduction. This arrangement was for the school year 1929-1930. At a previous time I taught for a short period Brother Morrison's class in Homiletics. Two years later, 1932, the college conferred on me the degree of Doctor of Divinity. I record these things here as they have some bearing on my relations with Pacific Bible College.

94

A few years later, in 1934, a group of ministers, principally in Ohio, became greatly concerned in that they felt the college was too slack in teaching the central truths of the movement. A very strong agitation spread widely through the church. It seemed the Ohio brethren were determined to do away with the college. As a member and chairman of the board of trustees I felt obligated to do what I could to heal the breach. I corresponded with Brother C. E. Byers, a leader in the agitation and a very good though excitable man, in an effort to find common ground from which to negotiate.

I asked the Ohio brethren to consider the possibility of dividing the college into a thorough Bible Training School more fully under the control of the ministry and to form the other part into a secular school less responsible to the ministry, perhaps located elsewhere. I approached Dean Olt also with the idea but he turned it down flat. Both sides seemed determined to win or lose but not to compromise. It was not that I favored the idea but I thought it might furnish a basis for negotiations.

Both sides were determined to win the fight. The Ohio brethren circularized all the ministers, and so did the college. A great homecoming was planned for the alumni. They were promised free lodging for coming to the Assembly. Also arrangements were made to ordain the graduating class of ministerial students so they might vote. This may not have been illegal but was quite irregular.

Brother Morrison was the center of controversy and the issue came to be his reelection as president. The showdown came with great feeling. Morrison was reelected with a majority of 13 votes. This settled the issue. Then followed an effort at understanding and reconciliation which well might have taken place earlier.

The college seemed to receive a new lease on life and soon was progressing toward a full liberal arts college. Dean Olt worked hard for this. He argued that even a minister needs a full four years of liberal arts training and the church wants a full liberal arts college for the benefit of all her young people. The program as outlined would not eliminate Bible and theology but would give them minor places. I said I believed the church would gladly finance the training of future ministers and religious workers but was not eager to finance the training of professional men, such as doctors and lawyers. But Dean Olt assumed to know what the church wanted. Perhaps he did.

Dr. Linn, who was one of Anderson's leading professors, and recognized as a leading biblical scholar in our movement, opposed vigorously Dean Olt's program. Dr. Linn insisted that biblical work should have the place of prime importance in the college. But Dean Olt won out and Dr. Linn resigned from the faculty.

In 1946 Anderson College became accredited and in 1950 there was added three years of seminary work for ministerial students. Several students from Pacific Bible College, now Warner Pacific College, entered the Seminary. A few of them told me that they took again work they had taken in our classes. This is not to say the Seminary does not do advanced work but only that they start at a lower point than where we leave off. Our purpose is to give to our ministerial students the most training we can in four or five years knowing that many of them cannot attend Seminary.

This calls to mind an incident in the experience of A. D. Kahn, a convert from Mohammedanism. Earnest efforts were made to persuade him to return to his old religion. This argument was used: "Our philosophy is that a man's life should be divided into three parts, the first part to be given education, the second part to getting wealth, and the last third to religion. Young man, proceed with your education and defer religion till later." Brother Kahn replied, "For all that I know I may be in the last third of my life now." And he was. Knowing that some of our ministerial students will not get to attend Seminary we wish to give them all the preparing we can while they are with us.

Though Anderson College is our oldest school with continuous service it was not long till there were others. In Texas Warner

Memorial was started but was unable to withstand the great depression. We have also Alberta Bible Institute, Gulf Coast Bible College, Arlington College and Bay Ridge Christian College.

PACIFIC BIBLE COLLEGE

The Northwest Ministerial Assembly, which consisted of the ministers of Oregon, Washington and Idaho, met at Spokane in September, 1935. The church in which the meeting was held joined the old Missionary Home, which was no longer in use. Ownership of the Home had fallen into private hands and had been taken by the County for taxes. It was in a run-down condition.

Brother J. J. Gillespie was planning to sing a solo so went into the old building to rehearse. He said to himself, "This Home was built by the church and should belong to and be used by the church." He expressed his feelings to others.

The need of a college was discussed by the Assembly. Brother A. J. Stuart reported on work that had been done at the Northern Rockies Bible School which he had founded at Billings, Montana. The good results of this effort were plainly seen. Brother Swinehart arose and said, "I move that we establish a college for the training of our young ministers." His motion was greeted with a wave of enthusiasm and was approved with an unaminous vote. I suggested that we invite our California brethren to join with us in the project. This we did but they answered, "not at this time."

A special meeting of the Assembly was held in Portland in January, 1936, at which time Brother H. A. Schlatter announced that he had secured in cash and pledges about half enough to redeem the Spokane Home. The Assembly decided to purchase this building for the college. A proposed curriculum was discussed.

At the next regular meeting of the Assembly, in September, 1936, a Board of Trustees was elected to proceed with plans for incorporating the college. This was carried out February 9, 1937. The original incorporators were C. W. Hatch, I. J. Masters, H. W. Smith, H. A. Schlatter, W. M. Donohew and A. F. Gray. The

Assembly met again in Portland April 6, 1937, and elected the same board including E. V. Swinehart under the new Bylaws.

After the college moved to Portland, in 1940, it became necessary to reincorporate under the laws of Oregon. The incorporators in this case were U. G. Clark, W. M. Donohew and A. F. Gray. The membership of the corporation consisted of the members of the Northwest Ministerial Assembly. The Assembly was enlarged to include California, Utah, Montana and Wyoming. Later it was enlarged to include the eleven western states. Then, in 1947, it was changed to the West Coast Ministerial Assembly with its membership thrown open to all ministers of the Church of God who were present, regardless of their residence. This group is the parent legal group of Pacific Bible College, now known as Warner Pacific College.

Chiefly through the efforts of Brother Schlatter enough money was raised to redeem the Home building ($700.00) and to make needed repairs. Brother Hatch, who was chairman of the Board, prepared our first catalog and Sister Daisy Maiden, who was secured to teach, cared for correspondence with prospective students. Thus they relieved me that I might accompany Brother Adam Miller on a missionary trip to the Orient. I had returned but a few days when we opened the school doors and began classes. This was October 5, 1937.

Our enrollment on the first day consisted of the following: Naomi Beasley, Evelyn Brown, Vera Hanson, George Kroker, Clarence Roper, Lloyd Sawyer, Wilbur Skaggs and Jewel Wemmer. These were regular students. In addition we had E. J. Fromviller and Anna Kroker as special students. Coming a little later were Allee Wilson, Mary Goble, Irene Kennedy, Margaret Bernard and Ray and Ronald Glessner. There were five others who enrolled as special students in night classes. This gave us a total of 14 regular students and 7 special students.

In the beginning of the school year Sister Maiden and I were the entire faculty. We divided the time between us so that she taught on Mondays and Fridays while I taught on Tuesdays,

Wednesdays and Thursdays. This arrangement was necessary as I still lived in Seattle where I was also pastor of the Woodland Park Avenue Church of God. This plan permitted me to be with my church four days each week. I employed Sister Myra Barrett to do visiting for me in my absence. I traveled back and forth between Seattle and Spokane each week, usually at night in a day coach. The N. P. Railroad furnished me a free pass.

Before the end of the first year Sister Maiden's father became quite sick so she returned home to be with him. Fortunately, we were able to secure Sister Mary Shepherd, who had taught at Anderson College, to take Sister Maiden's place.

Sister Maiden, in her younger days, had been a public school teacher. Also she had spent several years as a missionary in China and India. She was well qualified to teach such subjects as English, Christian Education and Missions. My teaching was chiefly in the field of Bible and Theology though I taught also psychology, Greek and Music.

For our second year Sister Shepherd was unable to return on account of ill health. We secured Sister Vivian Ahrendt to teach in her place. Also Brother William Schmuki came from San Francisco as a student and also to teach music. Sister Grace (Shoot) Donohew taught piano.

Having resigned at Seattle our family moved to Spokane in the summer of 1938. My wife Rosa became cook and matron. Together we received $100.00 a month and board and lodging for our family. No one ever worked harder around the college than did my wife. The first year Sister Kroker was our cook.

Our enrollment the second year was 31 regular students and 4 special students. At the close of this year we graduated our first class which consisted of Naomi Beasley and Allee Wilson. These two received the Christian Education certificate. The following year our enrollment reached 45. At the close of this year we graduated five. Evelyn Brown received the Three Year Ministerial Diploma and four others received the Christian Education certificate.

Sister Shepherd returned to our faculty at the beginning of our third year. But she was permitted to teach only a few weeks as she suffered a stroke of apoplexy and lived but a few days. In the same year one of our boys who sang in our male quartet was thrown from his bicycle and died from the effects of his injury.

Our college had grown to the point where our two-story house, about 40 feet square, with full basement was not adequate for our needs. Many of our students were rooming out. We needed more room and there was not sufficient adjacent ground available to meet our need. We concluded that if we were to move it would be advisable to seek a more central location. We thought a location somewhere in or near Portland would be ideal. A group was appointed to search for a new location. We found a few locations that seemed ideal but we did not have funds with which to develop them. Finally we discovered a large 40 room building that had been a sanitorium, repaired and vacant that could be purchased for $14,000.00 including 1.88 acres of ground. A meeting of the corporation was called and it was voted to prrchase the property.

On account of moving to Portland school opened a little late that fall, 1940. Miss Ahrendt was no longer with us but we added Miss Pearl Lewis and Miss Lottie Franklin to our faculty.

After moving to Portland from Spokane the college enrollment continued to increase till in a few years it reached 200 and in twelve years it was approaching 300. Students were enrolled from more than half of the States and from some foreign countries. Our graduates were scattered widely including foreign fields so that at one time more than half of our foreign missionary force had attended Pacific Bible College. The Board of Home Missions used several of our graduates also. The Church of God Year Book of 1957, the year I resigned as President, listed 175 of our former students which number had grown to 200 by 1965.

We arrived in Portland with assets of about $2,000.00. We purchased our property with a small down payment and reduced our debt rapidly. We arranged for a "Victory March" at the 1943

Northwest Ministerial Assembly. We used as our slogan, "Debt free in '43." We reached our goal and burned our mortgage. Thus in less than three years we could claim our original building as our own.

We continued to hold annual "Victory Marches" through which means we were able to purchase most of the property between 66th Avenue beyond 69th Avenue and between Mt. Tabor Park and Division Street with exception of most of the properties facing Division. In the year of 1946-1947 we constructed our first new biulding which was Pearl Lewis Hall accommodating 84 women and a matron's apartment. The building contains also a large dining hall. At the same time we received through War Surplus a building 25' x 125' which we used as our chapel. This building was delivered to us and reerected by the government with very nominal expense to us.

The greatest achievement of our early days was the securing of Dr. Otto F. Linn to join our faculty and become our dean. He had visited us in Spokane and expressed approval and encouragement when he saw what we were doing. I well remembered his withdrawal from the faculty of Anderson College and knew why. When he saw that our aim was to make the Bible and religion our central teaching he was well pleased. We tried at that time to interest him in coming to our college but he would give us no promise. However in 1942 he joined our faculty as dean.

Dr. Linn was a great Bible scholar, probably the best in our movement. His ability was widely recognized in that he was appointed on a committee connected with the production of the Revised Standard Version of the Bible. He served also on a continuing committee on collating Greek Manuscripts until his health failed.

Dr. Linn was also a humble saint with a pure heart. I worked with him in college administration for 13 years with fine cooperation. I have said we got along together better than Paul and Barnabas did.

Dr. Linn and I were confident we were carrying out the

wishes of the church in the Northwest, as well as our own convictions, in making of Pacific Bible College primarily a school for the training of ministers and church workers. Our purpose was published in the Gospel Trumpet as follows: "Regardless of whatever else it may do, *the primary teaching responsibility of the church is to teach religion* . . . Knowing that its facilities are limited, Pacific Bible College has committed itself to this one thing—religious training. True, the college teaches history, English, psychology, and similar subjects, but always with one object in view—the training of young men and women for definite religious service. Five years of work are given and two baccalaureate degrees are conferred. In all courses the major must be chosen in the field of Bible, theology, or religious education, and the minor likewise in one of these fields, or music."

In the same issue Dr. Linn states: "The rapid growth of Pacific Bible College indicates a warm appreciation for the service it is rendering. Of our two hundred registered students, ninety-two are definitely preparing for the ministry. This ranks Pacific Bible College with the larger theological schools of the country.

"Since our Bible is a translated book, the student who would know the full meaning of its contents must master the original languages. At present Pacific Bible College is giving sixteen hours of work in Greek language, plus two years of interpretation work based on the Greek text. Thus in four years the students may cover the entire New Testament in the original language.

"The Bible is the center of our educational program—this College is in fact as well as in name a Bible college. In biblical literature the College offers thirty-seven hours, with other courses given as occasion demands.

"The theology department organizes the contents of the inspired Book into a system of Christian faith. Theology is basic in life. Not only does it clarify the minister's thinking and give him respectable convictions, but it also helps him to lead others.

In our Department of Christian Theology we offer eighteen hours, and in the Department of Practical Theology fourteen hours.

"Pacific Bible College offers thirty-one hours of work in religious education besides the four credits in practical work that are required of all who major in this field." (The hours mentioned are semester hours.)

Thus it can be seen the College presents a full Bible program.

Largely through the efforts of Dr. Linn the College secured from the Oregon State Board of Education, in 1943, the right to confer the degree of Bachelor of Theology, and a year later the degree of Bachelor of Arts. Also the National Selective Service Headquarters, Washington, D. C., recognized us as coming "within the definition of a theological or divinity school," which gave our ministerial students 4D classification. We were approved also for the training of foreign students.

At the close of World War II we received a considerable number of students under the GI educational bill. This increased our enrollment for a time which was followed by a small decline as their training was completed.

For its first ten years Pacific Bible College was operated and supported almost entirely by the churches of the Northwest. In the year 1947 we were included in World Service. This is the story.

In the early 1920s there were five boards with offices at Anderson, Indiana. Each of these boards did its own promotion and as a result there was much duplication. Pastors were annoyed with so much mail and much of it went into the waste basket. So the five boards formed what was called the Associated Budgets. Brother R. L. Berry was chosen as secretary. Promotion was carried on unitedly with funds being divided proportionally. This arrangement was developed later into World Service.

In his promotion Brother Berry represented the five boards as children, the church being the mother. She must love them alike and care for their separate needs.

When the Northwest Ministerial Assembly created Pacific

Bible College a new board came into existence. I wrote Brother Berry thus:

"Get out the paregoric bottle, oil up the safety pins for there is a new baby. True, she was not born in the front parlor but in the back bedroom, but she is nevertheless a legitimate child of the church." Brother Berry replied: "Hurrah for the new baby. I had been expecting this but did not know when it would happen." The brethren at Anderson had no part in bringing Pacific Bible College into existence, nevertheless they gave us their blessing.

In a few years the baby college had grown to quite a child. As we were drawing students from and sending graduates to many of the states it was evident we were no longer a strictly local institution. In the year 1947 the General Ministerial Assembly, by official action, recognized our College as "an institution of the church doing work of a general nature." The way was opened for us to become a part of World Service. To do so would bring us under the control of the Assembly so far as budget and promotion was concerned. We were to cease most of our promotion for funds and to share in general receipts like the other boards. Our share would be about 6% the first year which, if the full budget was raised, would amount to about $30,000. We were not sure that we would gain financially by entering World Service as our western brethren were supporting us generously and hereafter funds received from the church were to be reported and leveled against. Our interest was in the field of cooperation rather than being financial. However our relations with World Service were very satisfactory for a few years but in time a serious clash occurred, which was like this:

The Commission of Revision and Planning, appointed by the General Ministerial Assembly, made plans for strengthening the organization. Among other things it decided Pacific Bible College should come under the complete control of the General Assembly like the other boards in World Service. We were willing to be so controlled so far as the budget and promotion was concerned but we were opposed to submitting our entire organization to the General Ministerial Assembly. But the Commission insisted that we must decide whether we were to be a sectional or a national school. This was not the real issue for the fact that we were a national school had been recognized years before by the Assembly. The issue was whether we would recognize the superior authority of the General Ministerial Assembly. This I refused to do.

I fought the demands vigorously, which were that our trustees must be elected by the Assembly and the election of our president ratified by them. Also that our constitution must not be amended without the concurrence of the Assembly.

I fought on spiritual grounds. Our Northwest Ministerial Assembly professed to be "in fellowship and doctrinal unity" with the General Ministerial Assembly for identification purposes. But we have never admitted that the General Assembly has any organizational or governmental authority over any body within the church except itself and boards of its own creation. I claim that any body of ministers have equal right to establish such boards as it may wish and such are not necessarily sectional but may be "national" as is anything originating at Anderson, if it is indeed national in its service. The Missionary Society is not under the Assembly.

I fought on legal grounds also. I held that as Pacific Bible College was an Oregon corporation with its place of business set as Portland that such important business as the election of trustees should be done by its corporate members in their annual meeting. I was sure we were better qualified to select trustees than were the members of the General Assembly. But the Commission was adamant. I inquired of the Oregon Corporation Commissioner whether our elections could be held in Indiana. He pondered the matter for a few days then decided it would be permissible.

Although these requirements went far beyond anything that had been asked or agreed to when we joined World Service our

Board of Trustees agreed to them and our Articles of Incorporation were amended accordingly. Thus Pacific Bible College came under the full control of the General Ministerial Assembly in 1956.

While Pacific Bible College, or Warner Pacific College, as it is now called, is under full control of the General Ministerial Assembly I still maintain that this Assembly has no organizational, administrative or ecclesiastical control over the church or the movement. Any other Assembly, such as the Midwest of West Coast, or even state Assemblies, has power to do anything Anderson can do. If in attempting to organize the "work" of the church we imitate the organization of others we will find it increasingly difficult to distinguish between us and the organized sects the movement was born to correct. An easy way out is to keep still about organized sectism.

After fifteen years of steady work for the college, with only two weeks absence on account of sickness, the Board of Trustees granted me a year's absence through the school year of 1952-1953 that I might spend a year in Africa for the Missionary Board. This year is reported elsewhere.

Upon my return I was soon in the click of things. During my absence Dr. Chapman was acting president. Plans were made for our new Library building as we were required to vacate our quarters then in use.

About this time our brethren in Southern California had located a vacant property at Riverside belonging to the Neighbors of Woodcraft which was for sale. It seemed an ideal place for a multiple purpose including sufficient buildings for the College and ample campmeeting ground and facilities for the World Evangelism program sponsored by the Southern California Ministerial Association. Brothers Chapman, Gough, Wade and myself went down to investigate and were well pleased with the prospect. The California brethren offered to sell their campground which they valued at $100,000 to invest in the project. We had not received a firm statement of the price except that it would be a bargain. After consultation with the California brethren we proposed to suggest an offer of $550,000 for the buildings and 25 acres of ground to be paid as follows:

Acceptance of our Portland property	$200,000
Cash down payment	25,000
To be paid July 1 (about 6 Months)	25,000
Remainder on a 20 year loan	300,000
	$550,000

Our suggestion was rejected. They would not accept our Portland property and their full price was quoted to us as $1,000,000.00. As this was entirely out of our reach we dropped the idea and began at once to construct the Library which was completed and dedicated to Otto F. Linn in November, 1954, at a cost of $126,300.00. Two years later we built the Men's Dormitory to house 48 men at a cost of about $100,000.00.

In January, 1955, a great celebration was held called Founder's Day. This was a combined college and ministers' celebration. Its main feature was the celebration of my fifty years in the ministry. Dr. Phillips, Editor of the Gospel Trumpet, was the featured speaker. I was asked to repeat my first sermon, which I attempted to do. A lot of honors were bestowed on me with a pylon erected in my honor. A beautiful chair and lamp were presented to me. Several songs that I had written were sung by the choir.

June 17, 1959, my wife Rosa and I celebrated our golden wedding. This was a happy time in which many of our friends expressed their congratulations. Rosa's health had begun to fail which saddened an otherwise happy occasion.

Dr. Linn and I realized that eventually we must step aside leaving our duties to others. We were praying and looking for others who might take our places. Our minds centered on Milo Chapman and Louis Gough. Both of these brethren were known by us and highly recommended. Brother Chapman joined our faculty in 1950 and Brother Gough in 1952. The failure of Dr.

Linn's health required that he resign his position sooner than had been expected. In 1955 Brother Chapman was chosen to succeed Dr. Linn as Dean.

The loss of Dr. Linn was a serious blow to the college. Most of our progress and development was due to his skill and effort. Although the college was not yet accredited it was moving in that direction. Dr. Linn would say we desired accreditation if it would not cost too much. He meant departing too much from our original purpose. Several of our students transferred to accredited colleges, both private and State supported schools. Usually their credits, such as would apply to their course, were received conditionally and in most cases were given full credit, thus establishing the quality of our work.

As a considerable number of our women students desired to become public school teachers Dr. Linn was able to make arrangements with an Oregon teachers' college whereby we could give the preliminary training, all but 17 hours, required to enter the teaching profession. This would require only a slight addition to our curriculum.

Since there is a growing feeling these days that a college education is a must, high school graduates are urged to go on to college and are always admonished, "Be sure the college is accredited." Also there is a widespread feeling that the duty of the church does not end with the training of its spiritual workers but extends to all of its young people.

These sentiments have pushed Warner Pacific College in the direction of accreditation and of becoming a full-fledged liberal arts college. This broadening does not necessitate that religion be given a smaller place. The administration of Warner Pacific College pledges that the religious department shall not be weakened.

In the year 1956 I was reelected president for another five year term but as I was 70 years of age and being faced with the problem of accreditation I suggested to the trustees that this might be a good time to change leadership as Brother Chapman was much better qualified than I to handle the matter of accreditation. This would require securing a dean. Correspondence was had with one of our former professors without the desired result. Also Brother Chapman needed more time in graduate school to complete work for his Th.D. degree, so it was decided to defer any change in administration.

A year later Brother Chapman had received his degree and was ready to assume the duties of president. I resigned and Dr. Milo L. Chapman was elected president.

After serving one term, five years, Dr. Chapman declined reelection as he much preferred teaching over administration. In the meantime Dr. Louis F. Gough, who had taught for some time in the Anderson Graduate School, returned to the campus of Warner Pacific College as Assistant to the President. It was natural that he should be chosen to succeed Dr. Chapman as president.

Within Dr. Chapman's administration provisional accreditation was received and construction of the gymnasium was begun. The gymnasium was completed and full accreditation received in Dr. Gough's administration. A new co-educational dormitory was built with other improvements and extensive plans for improvement to meet the needs of rapidly increasing enrollment were made.

Looking backward through the twenty-five years since Warner Pacific College moved to Portland much progress is observed. We began with our one building and less than two acres of ground. Our campus has been enlarged through the addition of several parcels of ground including a few houses. Also we have constructed five new buildings and have done some nice landscaping.

But it is not the physical plant that most fully expresses the value of an institution. The value is expressed more in the kind of contribution the college has made to the spiritual and intellectual development of its students, and its contribution to the well being of society.

Warner Pacific College is fortunate in securing an excellent faculty. Its first great asset was the securing of Dr. O. F. Linn as Dean. He was a scholar of high order having received his Ph.D. in the School of Religion of Chicago University. His scholastic excellence received wide recognition. Others added through the years include Warner Monroe, Mack and Irene Caldwell, J. W. V. Smith, Milo Chapman, Louis Gough, Orval Kerr, Kenneth Crose, Wilma Perry, Leslie and Nina Ratzlaff, Lauren Sykes, and others. These have served well.

From among our graduates many have become ministers and several are missionaries. Some have become college or seminary instructors while a goodly number are engaged in secular education or business. A large proportion of our graduates are giving a good account of themselves in filling important positions and rendering good service to mankind.

I believe this college has made a valuable contribution to the church and to the welfare of society. It is my hope and prayer that its good service may continue while time lasts.

My association with Pacific Bible College extended from its beginning till the spring of 1960 at which time I withdrew and moved to Seattle on account of my wife, Rosa's, serious sickness. Our daughter Lois had asked us to move in with her family so she could care for her mother. But the task became too burdensome for Lois so we returned to Portland and Rosa was placed in a hospital for a few months. After some apparent improvement we brought her to Dorothy's home where we cared for her till her death, January 24, 1961.

Immediately after the funeral I returned to Seattle with Lois and her family. Through the next year I shifted about somewhat staying with Lois part of the time, with Harold in Portland and with my brother Will in Seattle. Also I served for a time as supply pastor at Yakima and later at Grants Pass. Also I held short meetings at Bow Lake in Seattle, and at Woodburn and Ashland in Oregon. I attended the ministers meeting at Seaside and dedicated the new tabernacle on the Colfax campground. So I was not entirely idle.

As the weeks went by I became more and more lonesome. I was batching in one of Will's apartments. Nellie suggested I might do well to find an elderly couple to live with. I asked what need I would have for a man as I thought a woman would be sufficient. She and Will thought this a good idea and named for me a few eligible widows. I glanced about a bit and decided I would like to have Sister Farrell. I called to see her at her place of busines and made an excuse to come back. I suggested to her the idea of our marriage and found her quite willing. We were married Easter Sunday, 1962. For a honeymoon trip we attended the Anderson campmeeting returning through Canada.

ALBERT F. AND ANNA M. GRAY

Before our marriage we visited Portland and picked out a house which I purchased. Immediately after our marriage we moved to our new home, 2045 S.E. 72nd Avenue, where we lived two years. Later we sold this house and bought another more to our liking at 2534 S.E. 87th Avenue, 97216.

From the first day that Pacific Bible College opened in 1937 till the close of the school year in 1960 I taught classes along with my administrative work. In that time I have missed only two weeks on account of sickness; this was in 1948. I was absent during my sabbatical year, 1952-1953, while I was in Africa, sent by the Missionary Board. I have been absent also on business trips for the college or the church. Otherwise I have lost no time.

During these years I have taught many subjects, perhaps 20, ranging from music and homiletics to logic and Greek. My principal teaching was in the field of Bible and theology. I have not claimed to be an expert in any line but have been ready to do my best as my services were needed.

After our return to Portland Dr. Gough asked me to return to the faculty to teach a course in Systematic Theology and one in Church of God Doctrine. I taught these courses in 1963-1964 and again in 1964-1965. I will continue so long as I feel able and my services are needed.

During my three years absence from the college there have come many improvements. These are in physical equipment, enlarged curriculum and in increased faculty. There is much room for further improvements the realization of which will require much faith and hard work. Financial needs are great but so long as the college can keep God's blessing the future is assured. This, together with public respect and good will, spells success.

HEALINGS AND MIRACLES

Although I have taught and practiced divine healing all of my ministry I have never thought of myself as a specialist in this field. I have seen a number of healings and answers to prayer but not as many as some other ministers. I will relate a few that have come under my observation.

A Mr. Hickman, who lived in Spokane, was injured seriously when a pile of sacked flour fell on him. He was paralized from his waist down and suffered internal injuries preventing him from sleeping. Though I was a young preacher, just starting, when I heard of his need I called on him. He had not slept for two or three days. I did not have faith for the healing of his paralysis but I did believe God would heal his internal inqury so he could sleep. I talked with him trying to arouse his faith. In my confidence I said, "God will heal you so you can sleep." He replied, "I suppose he can." I said, "He will heal you now if you will let him." He said, "Do you think so?" I answered, "I know he will." My boldness caused him to ask me for prayer.

Immediately after prayer I left him to go to prayermeeting. A day or two later I visited him and he told me, "Immediately after you left I fell asleep and slept till some other company came and when he left I fell asleep again and have no trouble sleeping. God has healed my internal injury."

The church continued to pray for the healing of his paralysis. One day as I visited him his foot moved. I do not know whether his body became entirely well as I lost contact with him. Al-

112

though I have prayed for others many times it is not often that I feel the same boldness I experienced on that occasion.

In the spring of 1908 Brother W. S. Wade, a traveling salesman, took me with him on a trip to Craig Mountain, which is really a big plateau. We stopped over night at a farmer's home and naturally we talked about salvation and healing. The farmer told us of a lady who lived not far away who was very much in need of healing. The next morning we drove to her home. She was Mrs. George P. (Anna) Patton, who lived with her husband and two small boys near Ilo, Idaho. We entered the house and talked with her first about salvation and found that she was a good Christian. Then we talked with her about healing and found she had faith to be healed. We did not inquire as to the nature of her affliction. As she sat on a lounge we anointed her and prayed for her healing. Before I had finished praying she clapped her hands and cried, "I'm healed, I am healed!"

Three months later Sister Patton attended the Colfax camp-meeting and was sanctified and baptized. It was then that I learned the nature of her disease. She had what the doctor called tuberculosis of the bone. Decayed bone had been removed from her foot and hip. She spent sixteen weeks in a hospital at Lewiston. She was released and returned home but was far from well. Plans were made to return her to the hospital. She prayed that she might not have to go. The Lord seemed to say to her, "You will not have to go, I will help you out today." When she saw us enter her yard she was sure the Lord had sent us.

Before her healing her husband would have to be up nights with her but that night she slept well and continued that way. Within two weeks she had regained her strength and was doing all her house work.

Her husband was so pleased he gave up his tobacco and later was saved and baptized. Her healing was complete. She lived for at least fifty years after that, happy, serving the Lord, and enjoying good health.

A lady named Mrs. York lived at Asotin, Washington. She

was operated on for tumor. But when the incision had been made the surgeon discovered she had cancer in an advanced stage. The incision was closed without removing the growth. She was informed that the surgery had been successful though others were told she could live but a few weeks. Sister Little, learning about the case, sent an earnest request to the Assembly Meeting then in session at Moscow, Idaho, requesting prayer for her healing. Very earnest prayer was offered. As I was to make a trip up the Clearwater River in a few days and would pass through Lewiston the brethren asked that I should go on to Asotin and anoint the lady. This I did. But instead of dying the lady got better. Since his religion taught that the day of miracles is passed her husband would not believe she was healed. He sent her to a cancer doctor for an examination who reported that she had no cancer. A few months later this lady, now well, sent for us to come to Asotin to hold a meeting about which I have written.

While I was pastor at Clarkston we had a Sister Mitchell in the congregation. She was faithful in attending our services. One Sunday she was absent as her unsaved husband urged her to go with him for a trip. On the way their car was wrecked and she received a dislocated hip and a broken bone. The dislocation was set but in some way the broken bone was not set. She remained bedfast for some time. A series of special meetings were being held at our church and Sister Mitchell was brought to the meeting carried in a chair. At the afternoon service prayer was offered for her healing. She was timid about trying to walk just then but next morning she came from her bed crying, "I can walk, I can walk." She was able to walk without help even up and down stairs.

While holding a meeting at Southwick, Idaho, James Thornton was converted. He attended the services regularly till one night he failed to come. As he lived next door to the meeting hall a few of us, after the service, called to see what was wrong. There we found him sitting in a chair scarcely able to turn his head. He had worked that day in the rain and something like lumbago settled in his back. We talked with him about healing so, as he said later, out of love and courtesy he asked us to pray for him. In those days we nearly always knelt to pray. With great difficulty he got on his knees. We prayed earnestly for him and pronounced him healed by the power of God. As he attempted to rise he said, "My faith is not strong enough, I didn't get it." But as he continued to rise he said, "Say, I do feel better, it's leaving me," and as he reached his feet he exclaimed, "Why, it's all gone, well sir, what do you think of that?" He would sit, then rise and pick up his chair and say, "Well sir, how about that?" This was one instance when the weakness of one's faith did not prevent him from getting healed.

Another instance occurred when I was pastor at Yakima. An old brother was working in his garden on a very hot day. He suffered something like a sun stroke. He was carried into the house and laid upon the bed. I was sent for to come and pray for him. I found him paralyzed on the right side. His eyes were closed, his mouth was drawn, and he could not lift his right hand. He was unable to speak. After prayer he immediately opened his eyes and spoke. He reached out his right hand to me and rose up on the bed and sat up. He was fully restored at once.

He, together with his friends who were with him, rejoiced for what God had done for him.

While I was pastor of the Park Place church at Anderson, Indiana, Evangelist F. F. Bosworth, whom I considered a very Godly man, held a campaign in our tabernacle at Anderson. On special occasions the crowds were large but the ordinary week nights were disappointing. Elsewhere he had held immense meetings where great miracles had been performed. For some reason, I do not blame him, this meeting was not up to par.

Brother Bosworth had been healed himself and he promised God he would preach on healing two nights a week, and I think he did. He prayed for many for healing and I doubt not that some were healed though I am not aware of any unusual healings among members of our congregation. I do not blame him for this for God has his own ways of working.

Among those who received prayer for healing was Sister Martha Mills, a widow about seventy years old. She received no help. But one day later, as I made a pastoral call at her home, I prayed for her in a very ordinary way and she received healing. She had suffered with rheumatism for years and was unable to kneel. After her healing she could kneel freely. Also she had suffered with heart trouble for forty years and found it very difficult, if not impossible, to climb stairs. After her healing she could go up and down stairs without difficulty. She had been partly deaf for years. One day her ears were opened and she heard plainly, but this relief did not continue. It did seem to show that her deafness was functional and not really constitutional.

Sister Mills lived well into her nineties and continued to have good health till she, like a ripened sheaf of grain came to the harvesting.

Though most of the cases of healing I have mentioned happened long ago this does not imply that God no longer heals. The sick are still being healed. I will relate a few cases that have occurred in the 1960's.

At our Oregon State Campmeeting prayer is offered for the sick. Usually a special healing service is held when prayer is offered for many who are sick. Some of these, though not all, are healed. At a recent service it fell my lot to pray for a brother while others stood in agreement. A day or so later the brother called me and said, "You prayed for me at the campmeeting and I am no better; I am in great need. What shall I do?" I encouraged him to hold on in faith. A few days later he told me he was entirely healed and would not need the operation that had been recommended.

A member of the staff of Warner Pacific College, himself a minister, came to me for prayer for healing. He said an operation had been recommended. A short time later he told me he was entirely healed and would not need the operation.

A young girl became afflicted with a disease that deformed

her spine. Her parents brought her to the church where a small group of us ministers prayed earnestly for her healing. The next day her parents observed that a partial correction had taken place. The disease seems to be rebuked though recovery is slow.

A brother and sister visited my home where she requested prayer for healing. A few days later they told me that she had been healed instantly of an affliction of two years standing and the symptoms had disappeared.

A sister told me that her son underwent an unsuccessful operation and was given but a few days to live. She had her pastor pray for him and in a few days he was able to attend church service.

DEMON POSSESSION

When mention is made of devil possession eyebrows are raised for psychologists, psychiatrists, and many ministers are inclined to doubt that there is in fact any such affliction. They offer other explanations of the phenomena, even in instances occurring in the ministry of Christ. It is very true that over-zealous persons have called some cases demon possession which were clearly due to physical causes as, for instance, some cases of epilepsy. It is my intention to state only the facts as they occurred and leave others to make their own interpretations.

Perhaps the first instance that came to my attention occurred at a Colfax meeting about 1904. I was not present in the room but was on the grounds and was acquainted with all the persons involved. There was a small man who weighed not much more than 100 pounds who was judged to be demon possessed. This small man lay on his back on the floor where he was held by seven men. One held his head (this was O. A. Chapman) while the others held his arms and his legs. Suddenly he broke loose and sprang to his feet saying, "I can lick the whole bunch of you." The only way they could control him was by rebuking the devil.

At the Daisy campmeeting in 1905 there was a woman present whom the ministers declared to be demon possessed. They labored with her attempting to deliver her but as yet without success when I saw a young man rush up, kneel before her, throw his hat on the ground and cry out, "I command the devil to come out of her." She looked at him, fire flashing from her eyes, and shouted, "Who are you?" The young man was so frightened he sprang up, ran to the woods, and did not come back for his hat till the next day. I do not recall whether the lady was finally delivered.

The most extraordinary case of deliverence from demons that I have ever seen took place at Orofino, Idaho, in my meeting there in the fall of 1907, which I have already mentioned. This meeting was held in the home of Sister Hunt, near the mouth of Whiskey Creek, because her sister, Mrs. Bell Dunlap, was at her home beadfast with TB. The first night, while I was preaching, Mrs. Dunlap let out a screech which sent a shudder up my spine. At the close of the service Brother Alteneder said to me, "That woman is devil possessed." I thought so too so the next morning I hold her so. She asked me to cast them out so I prayed for her but nothing happened. She waved her hand and said, "They are all gone," but I did not believe it.

I went to the woods and spent an hour in prayer. While there there was revealed to me as clearly as if one had spoken audibly that this woman was possessed with six demons. They were named to me as a religious demon, an adultery devil, an infanticide devil, (really I was not familiar with the term abortion so I called the third one an infanticide devil), a profanity devil, a lying devil and a temper devil. I went to the house and told her, in the presence of Sister Hunt, what God had shown me. Sister Hunt said, "She confessed those very things to me while you were out. She confessed she had committeed adultry with three different men and had attempted to destroy her unborn child." The other sins were clearly apparent in her conduct.

As she lay in her bed, well covered, I placed my hands on her body and commanded the devil to come out of her. There occurred a violent commotion in her stomach. I continued to rebuke the religious demon and to command him to come out of her. The

118

commotion rose up to her throat which swelled as with a large goiter. As I kept on rebuking the demon she gave a big belch. The swelling went down and she fell back on her pillow.

After she had rested awhile I said, "That one is gone, now we will go after the next one." Again I laid my hands on her stomach and rebuked the adultry demon and commanded him to come out of her. Again there was the same commotion and as I continued to pray and to rebuke the demon and command him to come out of her the commotion moved up to her throat which again swelled like a large goiter, and again, as I kept on rebuking the demon with my hand on her throat she gave a big belch and the demon was gone. Again she rested a while then we took the other four in order in the same manner and with the same results.

After the six devils had been cast out I said to her, "These are all that the Lord showed me. If there are more I do not know: but I will lay my hands on you again and rebuke the demon. If any other is there he will stir. Do not try to hide him but let him stir." So I prayed again, but all was calm. Then I said to her, "They are all gone: now repent and ask God to save you." So she called on God to forgive her and save her and soon sat up in bed rejoicing in God's forgiving mercy.

There were present in the house during this procedure a brother, a brother-in-law, a sister, and a few others. These scoffed at the idea of demon possession. But as they watched and listened from an adjoining room they became firm believers. That night I preached on, "Oh, taste and see that the Lord is good," and sang, "It is truly wonderful what the Lord has done." Every sinner present got saved that night except the brother and brother-in-law whose "faces gathered blackness" as they resisted the Spirit.

A month later I was called to Orofino to conduct the funeral of Sister Bell Dunlap who had succumed to TB. I was always glad that I had obeyed the Lord's leadings to go to Orofino.

At a meeting at Colfax a man prayed with such vehemence and pounding of the bench that Brother McCully, who was in a room below, said, "The demon is upstairs." A few weeks later I was with some other brethren when we found this man to be grossly immoral and demon possessed. As we began to pray for him he was on his hands and knees barking like a dog. As Brother Charles Walker prayed for him he began to vomit a brown colored substance. Brother Walker said, "The demon is there alright, here is his broth." The odor was so offensive Brother Walker had to turn his head. When the ordeal was over the man was almost too weak to walk.

A more recent case occurred at Anderson while I was pastor there. A woman who was hard of hearing came to us for prayer for her healing. But instead of receiving healing she became stone deaf for a time. Later, while living with one of our families, she had a very bad spell. She could see green-eyed demons with the faces of certain spiritualistic mediums whom she had consulted. She was fighting them. A neighbor came in and tried to hold her with a rope. When I arrived we had prayer and she calmed down at once.

At a later time this woman had another spell. Another minister was present with me. When we prayed she became totally deaf and dumb and blind and paralyzed on one side. But as we continued praying she was restored to her normal condition though she remained hard of hearing. I fear she did not receive spiritual help for her life did not show it. However after I had left Anderson I heard that she had joined a church in Anderson.

There are many mental cases today that can be relieved by the psychiatrist but doubtless there are also those that can be cured only by the divine power of God exercised through prayer and faith.

MINISTERIAL SERVICE ABROAD

Although I hav spent most of my ministry in Idaho, Washington and Oregon, with 7 years in Indiana, I have traveled quite a lot. I have visited 44 of our states and 6 Canadian provinces. I have preached in more than half of these, sometimes as the invited guest for a campmeeting or ministerial convention but sometimes as a mere visitor. I spoke about 20 times in the big tabernacle at Anderson before the snow broke it down.

My first trip abroad was in 1924 when I was invited to the campmeetings at Saskatoon and at Provost, Alberta. I enjoyed these meetings very much. Canada does not seem like a foreign country as the people are much like our western Americans. In fact many of them came to Canada from the United States.

I found a few things different. They thought that as I was from the United States I must have coffee. Their coffee was poor but their tea was excellent. I preferred the tea. Their mail boxes were painted red and their fire alarm boxes green, just the opposite of ours at that time. Our boxes list the hours when the mail will be collected; theirs state when the boxes will be cleared.

The immigration officers on both sides of the border were very pleasant. Our officers would ask, "Are you a Canadian or an American?" The Canadian officer would ask, "Are you a Canadian or a citizen of the United States?" He did not call us Americans for they claim to be Americans too: and of course they are right.

Six years later, in company with A. T. Rowe, E. F. Adcock and F. M. Higgins I again visited western Canada. This was a missionary trip in which we represented our two missionary boards. This was a memorable trip because of muddy roads and the making of many new friends among our Canadian brethren.

MY THIRD CANADIAN TRIP

My third trip to Western Canada took place in 1942. I was invited to be the speaker for the Alberta and Saskatchewan campmeetings. The Alberta meeting was held at Camrose where the Alberta Bible Institute is located. The meetings were held in a tabernacle and the Institute property was made available; also private homes were opened to entertain visitors.

At that meeting I had the privilege of working with several ministers among whom were Harry Gardner, Victor Lingren, Walker Wright, W. G. Ewert, Brother Semerau, Brother and

121

Sister Abell and Brother and Sister Babel. All of these brethern were of great help in the campmeeting.

In addition to regular services I spoke several times over the radio, by transcription. These brethren were making use of radio stations at Edmonton, Calgary and Vancouver.

One day as I was preaching two elderly gentlemen came into the service. One was Frank Cole, father-in-law to my brother George, the other was my half-brother Charles. Alfred Witheril, former husband of our deceased sister Nettie, came also. He lived in Edmonton and Charles lived at Brownfield. It was a great privilege to visit with them, especially with Charles who told me things about our father that I had not known before. This was to be the last time I would see either of them for in a few years both died.

In addition to attending the Camrose campmeeting I attended the one at Saskatoon. Among the ministers at this meeting were Brothers Busch, Heffron, Popp, Millensifer, a Brother Booth who had come to us from the Anglican church, and perhaps a few others. This was a very good meeting though not so largely attended as the Alberta meeting. I have passed through Western Canada since but not to conduct services.

In 1952 Rosa and I visited the campmeeting at London, Ontario, on our way to Africa. While in Ontario we visited the old home of my parents at Fingal where my mother was born and married. We saw the church where their wedding took place. Also we visited relatives at St. Thomas and Niagra Falls. Fingal is about 20 miles from London but mother told me that when she was a girl a trip to London was to be taken not more than once in a lifetime.

We were to go from London to Washington, D. C. so we bought our tickets and checked our baggage through to Washington. As we were starting from Canada our baggage had to go through customs at Washington. We arrived there on Saturday and were informed that customs were closed on Saturday and we must wait till Monday. But I was to preach next day and our good clothes were in the baggage. When I explained this to a customs official he became very helpful and got our baggage cleared for us.

This was not our first trip to Ontario. Shortly after moving to Anderson we made a trip through Ohio, Pennsylvania and New York to Niagara Falls returning through Ontario and Michigan. On our return from Africa we stopped also at Gander, Newfoundland.

I visited our neighbor to the south also but only at Tijuana which I visited a couple of times, once during prohibition when this Mexican town boasted the longest bar in the world. Long lines of cars were parked, mostly American. Liquor could be bought legally in Mexico and imported in one's stomach. At another time I looked over into Mexica from El Paso, Texas, but did not go across the line. The country looked hot and dry. The Rio Grande, which formed the boundry looked, at that time, to be a very small river.

This covers my travels in the western hemisphere as I have not visited South America.

A TRIP TO THE ORIENT

Korea, before the war, was one of the most fruitful mission fields in modern times. In the course of fifty years a half million converts had been won to Christ. The largest group were Presbyterians though other missions were represented. Among these converts were many deeply spiritual and intensely evangelical Christians.

Among these Christians there arose a group who had become very tired of sectarianism and were in search of the true church. Through diligent study of the Bible they came to a clear understanding of the church. They came in contact with some of our Japanese brethren and found that they were in close harmony. Our Missionary Board was made aware of this situation and the Board decided to send Brother Adam Miller, our Secretary, to the Orient to meet these brethren and also to visit the churches in Japan.

A few years earlier a Filipino minister, named Matias, had come in contact with our work at Montesano, Washington, and was burdened to return to his native Philippines with the message. This he did, going to his home city, Laoag, where he raised up a congregation. Before long he took sick and died. His son, Fernando, took up his father's mantle and carried on the work, opening another congregation also.

Our Filipino brethren in Washington were eager to help the work in Laoag and wished I might go to visit and assist them. Through their assistance, and that of theWomen's Missionary Society, the way was opened for me to go with Brother Miller.

It was July 17, 1937, when Brother Miller and I went aboard the President Jefferson, of the American Mail Line, at Seattle, bound for Yokohama. My family, and a group from the church, saw us off. This was my first ocean voyage. I had not been out of sight of land except on Puget Sound in a fog.

We sailed among the beautiful islands of Puget Sound to Victoria, B. C., where we stopped two hours as we took on more passengers and cargo. Then we sailed through the Strait of Juan de Fuca, which is always rather rough, into the broad Pacific. By night we had our last sight of land with nothing to see but ocean and sky.

On board were a number of teachers bound for a great convention at Tokyo. They were pleasant traveling companions. At Victoria we were joined by an Anglican minister. He conducted a formal church service the next day, Sunday.

As we were sailing westward we were told to set our watches back 42 minutes each night. The official time to do this was 2 A.M. One teacher, so we were told, found it hard to wake herself up at that hour. Most of us attended to this task on retiring. In 10 nights we had set our watches back 7 hours. Then we were told to set our time forward 24 hours which would give us Tokyo time. Knowing the hands would be at the same place most of us made the adjustment mentally. The result was we were 17 hours ahead of Seattle time.

When Thursday came we were informed that we were nearing the date line and the next day would be Saturday. Actually we reached the date line Friday noon which was followed immediately by Saturday afternoon. But the time change was made Thursday night so that I wrote in my diary, for Friday, "I did not live this day."

Another peculiar problem was that at the date line I was about 8,000 miles west of London whereas Brother Miller was the same distance east of London, or 16,000 miles apart when in reality we were in the same room. Here east and west met. When the Lord said he would remove our sins from us as far as the east is from the west I hope he was not thinking of this date line.

When we had crossed the date line the purser, who had learned that I was a minister, asked me to conduct the church service the next day, I read Psalms 51 and Romans 1:13-17 and spoke on the Power of the Gospel. We had a good audience and more than half of the people, including some officers, expressed appreciation for the message. As we were a short distance from the date line this was the farthest east I had ever preached, though I went west to get there. My most westerly sermon was at Juneau, Alaska, which was at the same time my farthest north. The most southerly place where I have preached was at Nairobi, Kenya, Africa. I have spread myself like a setting hen.

The weather was quite cool most of the trip across the Pacific. Much of the time the temperature stood at 50 degrees. There were fogs and clouds with some nice sunny weather. Also we had rain which caused me to ask, "Why do we need rain here with nothing but water, water, water, nothing but water everywhere?" I recognized it was needed on land, but why here? Then the answer came, "There is plenty of water but none to drink or cook with. If a sailor becomes stranded on this broad ocean lest he runs out of fresh water a merciful and thoughtful God will send him some in the form of rain."

During the cool weather the crew dressed in their blue uniforms. But one morning they appeared all dressed in white. The temperature quickly rose to seventy degrees; we had entered the Japanese Current. On Thursday we got a glimpse of land and then soon saw many fishing boats which assured us we were nearing Japan. We sailed on to Yokohama which we reached that night. We anchored outside the harbor and waited for day. When morning came we looked out our porthole and there framed in beauty was Fuji Yama. The quarantine officers came on board and finding no one sick authorized us to proceed into the harbor where our ship tied to the dock, our voyage thus far ended.

Soon the immigration officers came aboard to examine our passports. They did not carry guns but each had a short sword at his side which seemed to say, "Don't worry, if we cut off your honorable ears it won't hurt much." However these officers were very polite and friendly. They examined our passports, asked a few questions, and passed us.

Brothers Shimizu and Maekawa came on board to meet us. They had known Brother Miller when he was a missionary in Japan years before. They greeted me also and soon we became well acquainted. Both of the brethren spoke English fairly well and Brother Miller could speak some Japanese. Soon our baggage was cleared through customs and we were on our way to Tokyo, about 17 miles away. Brother Shimizu had secured quarters at the Y.M.C.A.

Brother Shimizu and Brother and Sister Tanaguchi ate lunch with us at the Y. The meal was some different from what I was used to having. First we were each handed a small wicker basket containing a wash rag wrung out of very hot water. This was to wash our hands and face with before eating. We were served soup, salmon and boiled potatoes. There were green vegetables also but Brother Miller warned me not to eat them. Then we had a soft drink and bananas.

After eating we visited Brother Shimizu's print shop. When I saw the many trays of Chinese characters I wondered how anyone could find the ones he wanted. We then entered the living room after taking off our shoes. After visiting a while we spent the afternoon seeing the town. We had dinner at a hotel then went to Brother Shimizu's church where a reception for us was held. Here again we took off our shoes and wore sandals that were too short. The reception included prayers, songs and speeches by the Japanese and response by us. This was the first time I spoke through an interpreter but I watched how Brother Miller did it and sought to do likewise.

Early Saturday morning, about 6 o'clock, Brother Shimizu came for us with a taxi to take us for a ride into the country. (We were told about 90 percent of the cars in Tokyo were taxis and the fare was cheap.) We approached Fuji Yama but clouds prevented us from having a good view of the mountain. We had a pleasant day seeing sights of Japan including a visit at Miyanoshita.

It was our intention to stop briefly in Japan then proceed to Korea. But the Japanese brethren were to have a ministers' meeting beginning Sunday to last four days and they wished us to stay, which we were glad to do. So we postponed our trip to Korea till our return from China and the Philippines.

About eight o'clock Sunday morning a taxi came for us to take us to Brother Shimizu's church where we both spoke a little. Here was a nice congregation including many children. Then we went on out in the country to Murayama, about 15 miles from Tokyo, where the 4 days ministers' meeting was to be held. We arrived about 10:30 and found a good crowd already assembled.

The meeting was held in a two story hotel. Upon entering we removed our shoes and put on sandals. But when we reached the second floor, which was the meeting room, we left our sandals also and entered in our sock feet. Some of the people were barefooted. The floor was carpeted with thick, soft straw mats which even sandals might injure. The room was about 20 x 40 feet and had no furniture except a table and bench for the speaker. The people sat on the floor with their feet under them. Brother Miller and I sat on the floor but we could not sit on our heels for long like these Japanese people did. Most of the ladies and some of the men wore kimonos. Most of the men wore European suits. They bowed profusely, with their heads to the floor, to welcome us when we came in.

The service opened with the singing of several hymns. I could recognize most of the tunes but not the words. Then there were several prayers followed with a sermon by a visiting evangelist who was not one of our own ministers but evidently a Godly man. There was no other service till 5 P.M. After this service the men removed their coats, pants, shirts and undershirts handing them to a servant girl who gave each a kimono. These they put on and went outdoors to cool off, for the weather was warm and sultry.

I was invited to change my clothes also but declined. These men and women walked around outdoors singing hymns. I went to the room assigned me but Brother Miller returned to Tokyo leaving me with only a few who could talk any English. I thought I would read a bit but the light was too dim to read by.

I decided to go to bed. On the mattress there were two heavy pads like thick quilts, one to put under and one over the sleeper. There was also a bolster and a thin spread. I thought the spread was all I would need. I removed my clothing, except my shorts, and covered myself with the spread. I tried to lock the door but there was no key so I put out the light and prepared to go to sleep. But suddenly the door opened and the light went on and two girls were there ready to make my bed for me. One of them brought me a kimono and insisted that I put it on. I was able to convince them I did not need the pad. They tucked the mosquito net about my bed and said something which I thought to be, "Are you alright now?" I nodded my head and they left but did not close the door or put out the light. I did this, removed my kimono and got back into bed. Presently one of the girls returned with a glass of water which she gave me, tucked in the mosquito netting and left. This time she put out the light and closed the door so I knew the ceremony was over. I went back to sleep.

It was arranged that I would preach the next morning at

6 A.M. At about five I heard signing and moving about so decided to get up. Someone called at my door to inform me the meeting would be at 5:30 so I hurriedly prepared and spoke on the church with Brother Maekawa as my interpreter.

The evangelist spoke at 9:00 A.M. on John 15. I could not tell what he was saying but the response of the audience indicated they were much impressed. He did not attend the 5:30 meeting but spent the time in prayer.

After we returned from Murayama Brother Miller obtained tickets for us to attend the meetings of the Education Association, one of which was a Japanese drama very well presented. The actors were all men though one of them played the parts of women. We also heard several addresses and saw demonstrations of mathematical genius.

On Thursday we took the train to Nikko which is about 100 miles from Tokyo. This is the location of one of Japan's most famous shrines. We hired a taxi for about $4.00 which gave us a 5 hour trip. We went first to the famous Shinto shrine. Here is a marvellously decorated building with several rooms. In the main room people squat on the mats before the large disk which implies pure spirit and reminds one of the spirit of his ancestors. Here the altar is covered with food for the spirits. Worshippers sit in contemplation and toss coins on the mat before the altar. Priests declare that the spirits do eat the food. We suspected the priests help. In the dragon room a large dragon is painted on the ceiling. When one claps his hands the dragon answers with a roar. We suspect it is but the echo. Here are the most ornate buildings I have ever seen. Some of the decorations are covered with gold. Before entering the temple the worshipper visits the cistern where he rinses the bad words out of his mouth.

After spending 10 days in Japan Brother Miller and I prepared to take the President Hoover from Yokohama for Shanghai, Hong Kong and Manila. Before going on board we visited Kamakura where there is a famous statue of Buddha. This is not the largest but is the most famous statue of Buddha in Japan.

129

We boarded our ship which left at midnight nine hours late. All day Sunday we sailed near the shore of Japan and reached Kobe that night. Monday forenoon we sailed with high tide through the Japanese Inland Sea. This was a pleasant trip sailing between the mountains and islands. It reminds one of Puget Sound but larger. We passed many fishing boats, sanpans and junks and two submarines which may have been headed for China. We passed Shimonoseki late at night and next morning found ourselves in the China Sea. There were about 1,000 persons on board the ship. Many of these were Chinese fleeing Japan because of the pending war.

We reached Shanghai Wednesday morning and docked on the Whangpoo River some distance from the customs dock. A small boat took us to the landing. We, with two other passengers hired a taxi to take us about. This cost us $3.60 or 90c each. We visited the Chinese section and saw how dirty it was. We stopped at two dingy temples and saw the worshippers with burning candles praying to their horrible gods. How I wished I could tell them about Christ and salvation. We passed by where men were digging ditches in a rice field and wondered why. Perhaps they were fearing invasion by the Japanese. Japanese soldiers had killed the watchman at a Chinese airdrome. Police killed these Japanese trying to arrest them. This gave the Japanese an excuse for reprisals. That day we saw 27 Japanese war vessels enter the harbor. They took refuge behind the International City where they could attack China and the Chinese could not shoot back. We left at 11 that night.

We had planned to stay at Shanghai a few days but all afternoon, Wednesday, the Japanese flagship sent out messages, which I could not understand, which, I think, warned our captain that the fight against China was about to begin and advising us to get out of the line of fire. At any rate our ship left the same day we arrived. On our way to Hong Kong we received word that the bombardment of Shanghai began at two o'clock Thursday morning, just shortly after we left.

As we sailed toward Hong Kong the sea became quite rough. It was feared we were running into a typhoon however the storm did not get that bad. Our ship anchored at Kowloon, a part of Hong Kong colony but on the mainland. At night the high hill of Hong Kong proper was well lighted and made a beautiful sight. The next morning I took the ferry to Victoria, the British section of Hong Kong. This was the modern and clean part of the city. I walked around some and saw people living on the street. I visited some shops and bought a few things to take home. A Chinese man who spoke good English followed me about and told me where to buy good silks. He also pointed out a tailor shop where I might have a suit made for $4.50 U. S. I told him I was leaving on my ship at 5:00 and would not have time to have a suit made. He assured me it would be finished and delivered on board the ship before sailing time, but I did not buy. I understand a few passengers did. While in Hong Kong I had a tooth pulled which cost me $10.00 Mex. which was about $3.00 U. S. The dentist was an American. I have left teeth in Washington, Oregon, California, Indiana, China, and possibly elsewhere. I hope Gabriel will not have to gather them all up on the resurrection morning.

In Kowloon on the "go down" are shops where fancy furniture is made. Here one could buy a beautifully carved chest for $6.00 U. S. The problem was getting one home as they were about like trunks.

Our next stop was to be Manila where we arrived Monday morning, August 16. We were in our room gathering our things when the ship passed Corregidor, which we hoped to see. When we came on deck we were already in Manila Bay. Here, protruding out of the water, were masts and funnels of sunken ships I suppose the ones sunk by Dewey in the battle of Manila, May 1, 1898.

As our boat entered the bay we were met by many boats of many kinds of flags waving, whistles blowing and bands playing. I suppose this welcome was not especially for Brother Miller and me and we were willing to share the big part of the honor with Manuel Quezon, the first president of the Philippian Commonwealth on his return from Washington. However Brother Karl Krutz, who formerly had been a missionary in China, was living in Manila and met us. We stayed at his home while in Manila.

It was our intention to go soon to Laoag to investigate our work there. We had difficulty making connections as Brother Fernando Matias, the pastor was away at Cogayan where he had started a new congregation and built a church building. He had taken very sick and was not able to return to Laoag at that time. Also his mother had gone to be with him. In his absence a brother named Narcisco Pascual assumed leadership. This brother has a B.A. from the University of Washington and had taken correspondence from the Christian College at Eugene. He had been a minister for the Christian Church before studying books on healing then he came with our group.

After a few messages, back and forth, it was decided that I should go to be with them on Sunday, the 22nd. Brother Miller thought it unnecessary that we both go and as this was one of the main objects of my coming I proceeded to Laoag on Saturday leaving Brother Miller in Manila.

In the 4 or 5 days we were in Manila we were the guests of Brother and Sister Krutz. They took us about to see the city and the surrounding country. We found the old Spanish city very interesting with its thick walls and its massive architecture, especially its large Spanish churches. Its streets were narrow so there could be little automobile traffic. One thing I saw in this city that might well be used in some places in America was this: At a sharp corner with buildings obscuring the vision there was placed a large mirror in such a position you could see through it if anyone was approaching from the opposite direction. There are places in most of our cities where such a device could be used to advantage.

One curiosity we saw was a bamboo organ about 100 years old. The priest played it for us. All the pipes were made of bamboo. The tone was not very good but it was quite a novelty.

It was while in Manila we experienced an earthquake. All at once the house began to sway and to creak. Brother Krutz said, "It is an earthquake." I had never been in one before so did not know just what to do. We went to the door and stood where we could leave if the house should start to fall but the house was not damaged. This was a quake of the sixth intensity, the most severe they had experienced since 1882. It was followed by another quake of the fourth intensity. A few smaller tremors followed. The main quake lasted 3 or 4 minutes. A lot of damage was done but no one was killed in Manila though in some places persons were killed by falling trees. I asked whether any chimneys had been knocked down. I was answered with a smile, "There are no chimneys in Manila." Manila is only 14 degrees north of the equator and needs no fire to keep warm. Cooking is done with oil. I wished to attend to some business and although "calesa" fares were cheap I preferred to walk. I found the temperature not too high but the humidity caused free prespiration.

It was about 7 A.M. when I left Manila by train bound for Laoag. I bought my ticket to San Fernando, La Union, which is the end of the line. From there I went by stage 100 miles farther to Laoag, a total of 315 miles arriving about 9 A.M. They called the stage a truck which it really was. It had seven benches running crosswise to hold six people each. But in order to give the driver room the front seat was allowed only 5½ people. Printed on the side of the truck were the words, "Capacity 41½ people." I suppose the ½ person would be a child. I think we had our full complement with chickens under the seats and with the baggage on top. There were no rest stations on the way so without a word the driver stopped the truck. The men got off and went behind the truck. When they got back on the women got off.

When we reached Laoag two brethren met me and took me to a hotel where they had secured a room for me. This was a rather small room with a 6 foot ceiling, an open window (just an opening) and iron bed with a cane spring(?) covered with a thin pad and a sheet with another sheet for a cover. It had a large wash bowl with a pitcher of water to wash with and a small pitcher of drinking water. There was a mosquito net surrounding the bed. Fortunately I had two pillows, one of which I put under my head and the other I used where it would do the most good. I was not entirely alone through the night for three small lizards kept me company hanging on the wall, however they did not intrude within the mosquito netting. It took me some time to become used to my bed and go to sleep but finally I made it. The next morning I had breakfast of something like oatmeal, not very tasty. But I had no complaint for bed and breakfast cost me one peso (50c). About 7:30 Sunday morning Brother Pascual came for me and took me to the place of meeting which was Brother Matias' house. On the way he showed me the Christian Church and a hospital operated by them.

The Matias home would compare well with those of the average families. It was built on high posts, 6 or 8 feet above the ground. The framework was of bamboo with the walls and partitions consisting of mats made of banana leaves. The floor was made of split bamboo with the round side up with small cracks between. The roof was of metal which was probably a city requirement to avoid fire as the country roofs were usually thatch. There were three rooms and a porch with neither roof nor enclosure.

Our service started at 8 o'clock with about 30 people present. After songs and prayers in the Ilocan dialect Brother Pascual introduced me as "The Right Reverend Albert Gray." I think this is the only time I have been called "Right Reverend." Nearly all of the people present understood English but for the benefit of 3 or 4 older people Brother Pascual interpreted for me in the Ilocan dialect. I spoke on the church of God and what it teaches as the deity of Christ, the atonement, salvation, sanctification, healing and unity. As I had only this day with them I gave them a full meal. The people listened eagerly and at the close of the service I prayed for about twenty for healing.

While I was speaking about sanctification I observed that the sister of Brother Matias and her husband were very eager and hungry so I addressed a few words to them personally. They seemed ready for the experience. First I prayed for all in need then Brother Pascual prayed in Ilocan. As he prayed I laid my hands on this young man and his wife and prayed God to sanctify them. I doubt not that the prayer was answered. The preaching was followed by a testimony service and the entire service lasted about 2½ hours till 10:30. As some wished to be baptized we announced a baptismal service for 1:30.

I supposed the Laoag River would be the place for the baptism but as it is a large river with some current Brother Pascual thought best not to go there. He told me he knew a brother who has a tank he might let us use. I went with him to see the tank. It proved to be a metal barrel that holds about 50 gallons. The idea was to place the candidate in the barrel, push him under while the minister stood outside. I told Brother Pascual we would go to the river.

There were six people baptized, three men and three women. Another woman wanted to be baptized but as she was living with a man with whom she was not married I advised that she break off this relation first. Had I known more about the case I might have advised differently. The Philippines being a Catholic country has no divorce. But people do separate and chose other companions without it being legalized. They do much as many people do here legally except there is no way to legalize the matter there. This woman's husband had deserted her for another woman. This other man had taken her and lived with her many years and reared a family. But there had been no divorce and the second marriage had not been legalized. Should she leave him now? and where should she go?

We went to the river for the baptism. The current was not swift enough to be dangerous so we had no difficulty. The candidates brought clothes with them into which to change after being baptized. A group of ladies surrounded the women while they changed and one man held up a large bath towel while he stood behind it to change. I waited to return to the house to change my clothing. I was asked if I would care to take a shower, which I declined. I took my wet clothes out on the porch to dry and there was girl taking a shower right in the open. She was embarrassed but needed not to be as she was well covered. These people bathe but a small part at a time.

Among the people who attended the services that day was a woman smoking a cigar. She was not one of our group for our women do not smoke. But many women in the Philippines smoke and they all smoke cigars whereas the men who smoke use cigarettes. Men can afford to buy them but the women "roll their own." They raise their own tobacco and roll their cigars in any size and shape they wish. I saw them about as slim as a pencil and nearly a foot long and as large as a broomstick and rather short. After smoking a while she may knock off the ashes, put the cigar in her purse and save it for another time.

Sunday afternoon I took the truck back toward Manila. We reached Vigan in the night and had a lengthy rest stop. Some of the people got off at once and others waited a while. Seated in front of me were a man and his wife with a small baby. He was a Filipino and she was an American. He got off the truck but she remained on. Seeing that I was an American she told me her story. She had been a student at the University of Nebraska and he also. They fell in love and were married against the will of her parents and friends. Through their marriage she lost her friends. He decided to take her to his home where she would be accepted. But his people looked at her as a strange animal the circus had brought in. She had no real home anywhere. She had been in the Philippines two weeks and was homesick to go back to Nebraska. Her baby was very dark, perhaps the next one would be white. Her husband seemed more attentive to a Filipino girl, who may have been his sister, than to his wife. This experience confirmed my belief that intermarriage of the races is not wise. Perhaps people should not feel toward other races as they do for certainly all should have equal rights but if God has made them separate perhaps He prefers that they do not intermarry. The decision of the Supreme Court that races cannot be equal while separate may not apply to marriage.

We reached San Fernando in time for the train to Manila.

Upon my arrival at Manila I went at once to the home of Brother Krutz only to find that Brother Miller had left already for Japan and had left me on my own to come when I could. It happened this way: On Saturday word came from the steamship company that the United States government had commandeered our ship to rescue evacuees from Shanghai and persons wishing to leave Manila were to take President Jefferson which was leaving Sunday. There was no way to get word to me as I was on my way to Laoag and there was no way for me to return in time if I could be reached so Brother Miller went on as directed leaving me to find my own way.

I went at once to the steamship office to inquire as to what I might do. I was told that the President Hoover would leave the next day, Tuesday, and that I could have passage on it. The Hoover would stop at Shanghai to pick up American evacuees and proceed to Japan.

Brother and Sister Charles Hunnex were on their way to Shanghai but were unable to land because of the war there. Brother Miller cabled them to come on to Manila and arranged for them to stay with Brother Krutz. They arrived Tuesday noon on the President McKinley. Later they would go to Laoag for a time. I was at the dock when they arrived. I was standing somewhat above them and wished they might look up so I could signal to them. I thought that if I had a British flag I could attract his attention. (He was born a British subject.) Eventually he did see me. Brother Kurtz was there to meet them and he took us all to his home where we visited briefly then he returned me to the dock and helped the Hunnexes through customs.

I boarded the Hoover about 4 P.M. and at 5 P.M. we sailed bound for Hong Kong. We arrived in Hong Kong early Thursday morning. I sent Brother Miller word as to my whereabouts and he answered for me to stop off at Kobe where he would meet me.

We remained in Hong Kong (Kowloon) all day Thursday, Friday and Saturday while Chinese longshoremen loaded 7,000 tons of cargo. They were not very efficient but finally all was loaded. In the meantime Chinese men swarmed over the ship and took possession of the deck chairs. In the meantime crews were busy cleaning and painting the ship. It is cheaper to have this done in China where wages are low, also the ship was tied up anyway so time was saved.

It was reported that there was cholera in Hong Kong so the passengers were warned not to eat meals in town. Our tickets included meals while in port but several of the crew had left the ship. My table waiter was gone, and so were some of the passengers. I had to wait to be fed and received poor service. Once the waiter brought butter but no bread. But the service was good while traveling.

After our ship was loaded we left Hong Kong bound for Shanghai where we were to take on evacuees. The sea was rough and warning signals of a typhoon were up, however we did not encounter the typhoon. Through Sunday the wind was strong and the air cool. On Monday, August 30, the sea was calm. Sailing near the coast of China we passed several islands and lighthouses. Japanese cruisers were in sight much of the time. Airplanes were flying about. These were to prevent any assistance from reaching China. The Japanese knew our purpose so did not molest us.

As we approached Shanghai, in early afternoon, our propellers were stirring mud as we entered shallow water so our boat stopped for a while awaiting a higher tide. We were at the bar caused by silt brought down by the Yangtze Kiang. Some of the passengers went on deck where we saw many ships, mostly Japanese, with airplanes flying about. One ship proved to be an Italian liner and a British ship, the Cumberland, was not far away.

As we stood on deck I noticed 3 planes flying in formation

headed in our general direction but thought nothing of it as planes were flying about frequently. But suddenly I heard the roar of a plane diving right at us. I could not see the plane as the ship's superstructure cut off my view. Instantly there was a loud explosion and a muddy water spout shot high into the air near the ship, I would judge about 50 feet away. Realizing we were being bombed the passengers started below just as a crew member called, "All passengers come to lower deck." We all went down quietly and orderly. I went to my room to put on my life jacket. Other passengers did likewise. A second bomb exploded on the other side of the ship which sent shrapnel through portholes and through life boats but did not pierce the armor of the ship. Many of the crew were resting in their quarters and some were wounded, two quite seriously, of whom one died. While still in my room another bomb dropped that shook the whole ship. It struck on the sun deck and tore a hole about 10 feet across. If it had dropped down the air duct or a funnel it might have torn a hole in the bottom of the ship. It struck very close to the air duct. It exploded in an upper deck cabin which, fortunately, was not occupied. It tore this room to pieces and broke through the ceiling of the cabin below in which a lady was doing needlework. She was not injured. We were told that no passengers were injured, then later that a few were.

I had heard that in time of danger sailors would call upon God to spare them. I thought, "Now I will hear some loud praying," but I heart none, only profanity. One man ran to me demanding, "Give me a cigaret, my wife must have a cigaret." But I had none. Finally he located one for her. One woman gulped down a glass of whiskey and several, in the dining room where we were sent, sat on the floor with their heads under the tables, a lot of scared people.

As we looked out the window we could see a Japanese warship coming toward us. A Catholic woman rushed to me and asked, "Are they going to sink us?" I replied that if they wanted to sink us they would not need to come so close. Then I asked her if she was afraid to die. She exclaimed, "I don't want to die; I don't want to die." I explained her life jacket would keep her from sinking but she was afraid the fish would eat her.

Another lady sat calmly in her chair. Her face was the expression of peace with no worry at all. I talked with her a while and learned she had been a Baptist missionary in China for 49 years. Her only regret was that she could not serve one more year and round out 50 full years of service.

As for myself I felt a calm peace within my soul through it all. I knew the Lord would take care of everything in his own way and I felt no fear.

After the bombing had ceased the people felt quite glum. We had missed dinner so we were served sandwiches and coffee. Then the Captain invited us all to the first class saloon. I thought he would make a few remarks of thanks for our safety and assurance that we were now safe. But instead an officer announced a dance and invited couples to come onto the floor. Only one couple came. Then he exhorted like an evangelist giving an altar call but without success. Then a man appeared with a bottle of whiskey which he passed around then the revelry began. I knew this was no place for me so I left.

Here I saw an example of man's depravity. In the time of deep danger God was not entreated: in the time of deliverance no word of thanks was offered Him. Does this not confirm God's word, "God is not in all his thoughts."

The final report was 6 sailors and 2 passengers injured. One sailor, a young man 23, dead. We sailed with the flag at half mast.

How and why did it all happen? This was the question on all lips. The officers offered no explanation except these facts: There were 3 planes and each dropped 3 bombs, 9 in all, with 3 taking effect. The planes bore Chinese markings.

The most common theory among passengers was that the Japanese had done it. They used Chinese markings so we would think the Chinese had done it and China would lose our friendship. Another suggestion was that it had been accidental, but this was hard to believe as a large American flag was painted on the deck and the (Dollar sign) ($) appeared on the stacks and could be seen miles away.

A German naval officer on board told me he was sure the Chinese had done it for the Japanese shrapnel was made of American scrap iron whereas the Chinese got their material from Russia. The shrapnel used was Russian, not American scrap iron.

The Chinese government admitted it was their fault. They had mistaken our ship for a Japanese transport bringing in soldiers. When they saw their mistake they ceased the bombing. They were asked to pay $500,000 damages, which, according to the value placed on the Hoover, was about ten times the damage done. I doubt it ever was paid.

The Hoover did not stop at Shanghai as had been planned but on account of the bombing proceeded at once to Kobe. I was to meet Brother Miller here.

Our trip from Shanghai was calm and uneventful. We reached the breakwaters of Kobe about noon on Wednesday where we waited for the quarantine officers to come aboard. They were to arrive at noon but did not come till 2 P.M. so we missed our lunch waiting for them. As the boat had come from Hong Kong where there is cholera they insisted on examining everyone. Then followed the immigration officers who examined everybody even though only two of us got off. We tied up at the dock about 6:30.

As our boat tied up at the Kobe dock a considerable number of people were present watching us come in. I scanned the crowd as I looked hard to locate Brother Miller but I could not find him. He was not there. I went to the customs office and had my baggage examined and passed. I found a taxi driver who could talk English and had him take me to the Y.M.C.A. where I was sure Brother Miller would look for me. I had difficulty in making the clerk understand that I wanted a room, but they had no vacancy. So I asked the taxi driver to take me to a good hotel. He took me to Hotel Fuji where I got a good room for 4 and slept well.

The next morning I went to the office of the Dollar Steamship

Company to leave my address in case Brother Miller should try to reach me. I discovered my ticket had not been properly validated so the agent advised me to return to the Hoover and have it attended to. The purser fixed it for me and told me he had a telegram for me. It was from Brother Miller telling me he had been delayed but would arrive on the train that evening. So I had the day to loaf about not knowing a person who could speak English and I could speak no Japanese.

I went to a restaurant to get a meal. The menu was in Japanese and French but I could read neither one. I took a chance and ordered something. I made it alright.

As I walked about I saw a street carnival and walked around in it. As I passed a shooting gallery a girl addressed me in good English, "Come on, try your luck." Soon a man carrying a package stopped before a wayside Shinto shrine. He laid down his packages, jerked a rope which rang a bell, clapped his hands, apparently to get the attention of the spirit, then offered a prayer, rang off with another handclap, and went on. I met Brother Miller and took him to my hotel where we rested well that night.

It had been our plan to meet some of the Korean brethren at Shiminosoki but it was very difficult for Koreans to enter Japan. Passports were required and not easy to get. But as Japan then ruled Korea the Japanese might enter Korea at will. So the Korea brethren requested us to come to Heijo (Pyongyong) and meet the brethren there. Brother Shimizu met us at Kobe and together we traveled by train to Shiminoseki. That night we took the boat to Fusan (Pusan). On the boat we were interviewed by customs, immigration and police officers. When we arrived on the dock at Fusan a Korean officer, Mr. Lee, stepped up to me as I followed Brothers Miller and Shimizu and said, "You will go with me to the police station." I didn't know why so I said "I am with these men." He answered, "I know, they are going too." We were to have our passports and papers inspected. We were passed without difficulty. They asked what we would say about the war. I replied, "We are Americans and neutral. We will not discuss the war." They said then, "Will you pray for us?" We promised to do that. We learned Mr. Lee was a good Christian, he had been to America and attended Wheaton College.

At Fusan Song San, editor of The Cross, who lived in Keijo (Seoul), met us. At Taiden another brother, Nakahara San, met us. He was a Japanese. At Keijo we were to meet Brother Chung, an independent evangelist who had met us at Anderson a year before and reported to us about the work in Korea. He was to go with us to Heijo to be our interpreter but could not go. He agreed to meet us on our return but did not. We learned he had been accused of a part in an uprising 23 years before that, though he had no part in it, and had now spent 58 days in jail. He was released but not allowed to preach. Evidently this is why he did not accompany us. Japan was not too generous in its dealings with its Korean subjects.

We reached Heijo in later afternoon. As we got off the train we saw a long line of women dressed in white standing in line to welcome us. Brother Miller told me to look straight ahead and not to notice them. I did as he said though I did not know why. We went to the Railroad Hotel near by which, I understand, belonged to the Japanese government. Here we stayed over night, Brother Shimizu with us.

Next morning (Sunday) we took a taxi to the church. When we arrived the service had already started. There were about 150 people present which included most of the ministers in Korea. There were two doors to the church, one for men and one for women. The men sat to the speaker's right and the women to his left with an aisle between. As one might expect, there were more women than men. There were no seats for the audience so they sat on the floor on their heels. How they could do this I do not know. There were seats for the speakers.

Though we could not understand the words one could not help feeling the presence of the Spirit as they sang such songs as, "What can wash away my sins? Nothing but the blood of Jesus." The songs and prayers and response of the people thrilled

143

our souls. Seldom in America, or anywhere else that I have been, was there a greater spiritual power felt.

I was to preach that morning on the church. I preached as I do at home. The people responded well for God had led them into the same truth.

That afternoon we met with the ministers and Bible women. There were benches for the men but the women sat on the floor back by the wall. As there was some vacant room on the benches I motioned to the ladies to come and sit on the benches but they did not move nor did they take any part in the conversation. I learned social cutoms differ from ours without destroying spiritual fellowship.

Our discussion with these brethren was very profitable. We found no particular point on which we disagreed. They were hungry for our fellowship and would welcome our assistance and financial help. But they were fully committed to the message which they had received from God and were determined to spread it as fast as they could even if we could not help them.

Brother Miller spoke to them at the evening service informing them of the work of the movement in this country. His message was very enlightening for them.

Brother Miller and I were honored guests at a real Korean meal. There was plenty of such things as shrimp, devil fish, cucumbers, other kinds of fish, raw and cooked, and many things I cannot name. Brother Miller had a list of 30 things on the table. To try to meet our appetite there was included a boiled chicken without seasoning. We began our meal with chopsticks, but after laughing at us for a while (me in particular) they furnished us tools to eat with.

At the evening service as soon as Brother Miller finished speaking we hurried to the depot to catch our train for Keijo. Brothers Song and Nakahara were with us. We sat up all night and reached Keijo early while still dark. We took a taxi to Mrs. Kumabe's place. She was an American lady with a Japanese husband. The taxi driver was afraid to take us all the way so let

144

us off near the place. The law required inn keepers to report all patrons but as we had not stayed over night we were not reported, hence the police lost track of us.

Early that morning we met with Brother Song's church of about 50 people. The meeting place was in an out-of-the-way place not easy to find. Brother Miller and I both spoke briefly. Brother Shimizu served to translate into Japanese, then Brother Song translated from Japanese into Korean. Then Brother Shinizu preached to the group.

Brother Nakahara was acquainted with some government officials and was able to escort us sight seeing. So, after breakfast with Mrs. Kumabe and her husband, we visited the government buildings and other places of interest. This kept us busy till noon when we were to take our train for Fusan. The police had lost track of us but were at the depot ready to interview us again. They questioned our Japanese men who were with us, Brothers Shimizu and Nakahara. We were glad they did not know where we were early in the morning. I was unaware that Christians were allowed to meet only on Sundays and Wednesday nights. We were violating the law by having an early morning Monday meeting. Brother Miller seemed a little nervous but as I didn't know about the restriction I was at ease. What if the police had caught us at it?

When we arrived at Fusan our Mr. Lee met us. We reminded him that we arrived back at the time we said we would. We were examined again before leaving Fusan. This made no less than 20 times we had been interviewed by immigration officers and police in less than 3 days. Japan seemed jittery and afraid of spies.

In Kobe I saw a large American flag hung and under it the words, "America is our friend." This was 4 years before Pearl Harbor. However at that time they expressed freely their dislike for England.

From Fusan we took the boat to Shiminoseki. Curtains were drawn to effect a blackout. We arrived at Shiminoseki in the morning and were now quite free from police interference.

We took the train back to Kobe, stopping at Hiroshima to see Keiji San, son of our earliest missionary, Brother Yajima. He took us to see the famous torii which stands out in the sea. It had been erected on dry land but an earthquake, six hundred years ago, caused the land to sink. Here we visited a temple where soldiers bound for China were worshipping and praying for power to kill Chinese.

After our stop at Miyajima, the place of the torii just mentioned, we made our way back to Tokyo stopping at Kobe, Kyo-to (old capital) and elsewhere. At Kyo-to we visited an ancient Buddhist temple where we saw candles burning, priests chanting, and people using prayer beads which hung from their wrists instead of their necks which, otherwise, reminds one of a Catholic service. After a few other stops we made our way back to To-kyo (new capital) and again took up residence at the Y.M.C.A.

For the next few days Brother Miller and I visited several of the churches in Tokyo. Usually both of us spoke but sometimes we went to separate places. Brother Maekawa took me to a mission where a brother cared for people with TB and some were insane. This man had been an Episcopalian but Brother Maekiwa led him to us. Then on Saturday evening Brother Maekiwa took me to a place about 50 miles from Tokyo where I spoke in a private home on the parable of the sower. Some of those present had never before attended a Christian service. Then we went to a factory where 700 girls worked spinning silk thread. They are hired out by their fathers by the year and live at the dormitories. I was invited to speak to them. I spoke on "Consider the lilies how they grow," referring to the beauty of Japan and pointing out that man was God's most precious creation. But man had been defiled by sin and might be restored through Christ. All 700 girls were present and seemed to appreciate my message. Only 4 of them were baptized Christians. I learned that silk worms are kept in cages and mulberry leaves are brought to them for food.

Our last Sunday was a busy day so Brother Shimizu suggested

that I rest a while at his parsonage while he and Brother Miller visited another church in the afternoon. They let me off at the door where I removed my shoes upon entering. Sister Shimizu welcomed me but she could speak no English and I spoke no Japanese.

Sister Shimizu pointed to a seat and said, "Dozo." There, I thought, I have learned one word, "Dozo" meant be seated. She left the room and presently returned with a cup of tea and said, "Dozo." I thought, does "Dozo" also mean tea? I discovered I was not learning very fast. There was an organ in the room so I sat down and began to play a familiar hymn, and as I played in English she stood behind me and sang in Japanese. When her husband came home she said to him, "You left that man here who can speak no Japanese and I can speak no English; all we could do was to look at each other and smile." Then I learned, as I had never known before, the meaning of the song, "You can smile when you can't say a word."

The time was drawing near for us to leave for home. We visited, I think, all the churches in Tokyo. These have all been destroyed since in the war, except the Missionary Home at Hongo. There were farewell parties for us and a very friendly send off as we returned to Yokohama to take passage for San Francisco. Our boat left late and as we had a rough sea with strong head winds we continued late.

On the following Monday we reached the date line. Instead of naming Monday twice the ship called one Meridian day. Brother Miller argued that we had an extra day that week but I denied it holding that Monday was 48 hours long. I argued that on the contrary every day is 48 hours long. From the time it begins on the west side of the date line till it ends on the east side is 48 hours. We argued the matter most of the day and neither of us would give in. At any rate we gained back the time we lost going over.

We arrived at Honolulu toward night. We got off the boat and visited brother and Sister Baker who took us to see Waikiki beach. We returned to our boat for the night and sailed the next morning bound for San Francisco.

On our way to San Francisco we learned that a longshoremen strike was threatened and we might have to go to Los Angeles. But the strike did not occur so we landed at San Francisco as planned. When we entered the Bay a quarantine officer came aboard to inspect us. Two women did not want to be inspected so they kept hidden. This delayed our landing two hours. These two were not popular as everyone wanted off. A tug boat brought us to the pier and we were soon unloaded. Brother Miller and I continued by train to Portland where we separated, he went on east and I went to Seattle.

Thus ended our trip of 75 days in which we traveled more than 20,000 miles and visited, Japan, Korea, China, The Philippines and Hawaii. In all of these, except China, we visited our own people.

We found the Japanese people highly cultured, great lovers of beauty and very courteous. We saw no beggars in Japan but this is not to say none of the people were poor.

In Korea we found the people crushed under Japanese rule and yet these Christians were very courageous and spiritual.

China was overrun with poverty, filth and beggars. I cannot say which was worst, Shanghai or Hong Kong. People were living, sleeping and dying in the streets.

The Philippino people were about ready for freedom from the United States and were not sure they wanted it. One congressman said to me, "If it was not for the American flag what is happening in Shanghai might be happening in Manila." But the American flag did not prevent it coming later. Most of the people are poor but courageous.

Though our Japanese brethren were very courteous they told us they would welcome us to work with them but they did not need our leadership as they could direct their own work. Since the war they seem to have changed their attitude in regard to this.

TRIP TO AFRICA

At the Missionary Board meeting in 1951 there appeared a need that someone visit the mission station in Africa. I was asked if I might be available for the trip. After consulting with my wife we agreed to go. Inasmuch as I had taught at Pacific Bible College for fifteen years without a sabbatical leave the board of trusttes granted me a year's leave for the year 1952-1953. Milo Chapman was appointd to serve as acting president during my absence.

There were several things to do in preparation for the trip. We secured our passport and visas and took our "shots." We decided to ship what we would need in a fifty-gallon steel barrel. A box is too easily broken into and pilfered. Things needed on the way were taken in suitcases.

We went first to Anderson where we stayed during the campmeeting. As our ship was not due to sail for about a month we had hime to travel about some. We visited two churches in Dayton, Ohio. and also attended the campmeeting at London, Ontario. From there we visited distant relatives of my mother at Fingal and Saint Thomas in Ontario, and Niagara Falls, N. Y. From there we went to Washington, D. C. via Buffalo. We did considerable sight seeing at Washington. We visited the Capitol, White House, Washington and Lincoln monuments, Arlington and Mount Vernon and visited some museums. Also I spoke at the National Memorial church and one of our colored churches.

After a few days stay in Washington we proceeded to New York, stopping en route at Princeton, N. J., to visit the Goughs. At New York I spoke at the Grand Avenue church and accompanied the pastor to visit the Eastern campground in Massachusetts. We passed through Connecticut. This was my first trip to New England. I spoke to a small group at the campground.

While in New York we visited St. Patrick's cathedral, the Marble Collegiate church, the Riverside church and the Cathedral of Saint John the Divine which is said to be the largest cathedral next to Saint Peter's in Rome. Brother Wampler took us to an Indian restaurant where we ate rice and curry, then watched the production of a movie broadcast.

When the day of sailing arrived we were taken to our boat, the Khedive Ismail, which would sail from Hoboken, N. J. Brother Earnest LaFont and his family, were sailing with us. They were going to Cairo to join the missionary staff there. Brother and Sister Gough, Brother Harold Phillips, and a few others, saw us off.

As we left the harbor for the open sea we passed the Statue of Liberty which was a very imposing sight. Outside the harbor we saw a ship approaching but as night soon came on we were to see nothing but water and sky for several days. We sailed July 22, 1952 and were to disembark at Alexandria, Egypt, nearly three weeks later.

Ours was an Egyptian ship manned with an Arab crew. Most of the passengers were Arabs and not many of them could speak English. The food was different from what we were used to but we had plenty to eat. We could not read the menu but as the waiter brought food we selected what we wanted.

Friday being the Mohammedan sabbath the radio blared forth weird music most of the day. The words were Arabic so we could not understand but understand much was from the Koran. Nothing of importance occurred on Saturday, the Jewish sabbath, and I doubt that there were any Jews on board. On Sunday a Christian service was held. Brother LaFont had charge and I spoke about God. There were about twenty people present. One Egyptian said to me, "It is alright for you to go to Kenya but we have our religion and we do not need Mr. LaFont in Egypt." The other Sundays we were in port.

On July 30 we sighted the coast of Portugal and that night we entered the Mediterranean Sea. We wished to see Gibralter but we passed that point at 3:00 o'clock in the night. I did not get up to see it as I thought it too dark to see much. We found the Mediterranean quite calm and the air was balmy. Much of our way we could see the coast of Spain as we sailed toward

Marseilles, France, our first stop, where we arrived, Saturday, August 2.

Our son Harold was with the U. S. Air Corps stationed at Bordeaux. He met us at Marseilles where we had the day together visiting and seeing the city. With the LaFonts we ate at a nice restaurant. The waiter was much surprised that we refused the wine and asked for water instead.

Our ship left at 5:00 bound for Genoa, Italy, where we arrived Sunday morning. We spent two days there. We took a sight-seeing tour and saw much of the city which is very picturesque. One of its chief attractions is the galleries of "24 acres of marble." Here are statues of beauty honoring the dead buried there. We saw also the house where Columbus was born. There were many ships in the harbor but I saw few American ships. I wondered what is wrong with our maritime enterprise. Are we pricing ourselves off the sea?

From Genoa we sailed to Naples. Here we met Chief Childres who was assigned to the U.S.S. Adirondac which was anchored there. He is a brother to one of our college students. We could see Mount Vesuvius but had no time to go to examine the ancient ruins. We spent our time viewing the city and buying a few things.

From Naples we sailed toward Beirut which was to be our next stop. We passed between Sicily and the "toe" of Italy through the very stait Paul must have sailed through on his way to Rome. Also we "passed under Crete" as he had done, in the opposite direction.

As we "passed under Crete" we experienced, it seemed to me, the stormiest part of our trip. A raw wind was blowing and the sea was covered with whitecaps. We could see little of the island except rugged mountains though the interior may have been different.

After sailing the full length of the Mediterranean we arrived at Beirut, Lebanon, where we spent 24 hours. I went ashore and walked about some. I took a few pictures till a young man who could speak English told me I was breaking the law. I am glad no police caught me at it. Although Beirut was our most easterly call it was not the end of our journey. From there we sailed southwestward to Alexandria, Egypt, which was our destination. Here we arrived on August 11, after 20 days of ocean voyage. It had been a pleasant voyage even though the service and associations were not equal with that on American ships. I kept well all the way with no sea sickness. Rosa enjoyed the trip too though she missed a meal or two.

We were met at Alexandria by Brother Wilbur Skaggs and Brother Tobakian, the Armenian pastor. We took the ladies and children to Camp Caesar, the home of Brother Fleenor, then returned to the dock to get our baggage through customs. We had no difficulty in this. After visiting with Brother Tobakian at his home briefly Brother Skaggs took us in his car to Cairo, a distance of 132 miles. On the way we passed through desert country mostly. We could see camels moving about loose, though probably they had owners, and saw a Bedouin saying his prayers as he knelt toward Mecca, as he supposed, though I thought he was facing the wrong direction. But I doubt that it makes any difference. We arrived at Cairo about 8:30 P.M. the first leg of our journey completed. We remained in Cairo one week and visited the pyramids, and the sphinx and rode on camels. Also we visited a museum and saw much of the city. We stayed with Brother Skaggs at the Mission Station in Maidi.

We remained in Cairo over Sunday where I spoke to the Greek congregation and also at the Egyptian church. We had a conference also with the editor of the Arabic church paper who was somewhat out of harmony. Goodwill was reestablished.

We had planned to fly to Nairobi but received word from Frank LaFont to come to Entebbe in Uganda where we would be met. We were unable to do this as our passport did not include a visa for Uganda. We sent word to Brother LaFont that we would arrive in Nairobi Tuesday morning, August 19. We took the BOAC plane from Cairo Monday night. Rosa had not flown before but showed no anxiety and I think really enjoyed it.

Shortly after we were airborne a steward came through the plane with drinks. We asked for orange juice, grape or lemonade, but he had none. He offered us, (I thought he said cherry) a reddish drink. We thought cherry juice would be good so accepted. I had never before tasted such a horrible drink. I concluded he had said Sherry.

We arrived at Khartoum, Sudan, about midnight where we landed for a brief rest. A light lunch was served and then we were off for Nairobi. We arrived at Nairobi at 8:00 A.M. Whether we flew over Ethiopia or not I do not know. We went through customs and as no one was there to meet us I inquired for a message and was told there was none. We were taken to the BOAC office where I asked again, but no message so we went to the Norfolk Hotel. We sent a telegram to Brother LaFont asking instructions. As communications are slow we did not receive his reply till the next morning. He had sent us a message but for some reason I did not receive it. We stayed overnight at the hotel, then, upon receiving his message hurried to the railroad station and took train for Kisumu.

Before boarding the train I glanced at the time table which showed the train would leave Nairobi at 11:20 and reach Kisumu at 5:20. As the distance is about 240 miles that seemed to mean about 40 miles to the hour which would be a fair speed. But the train started out slowly. It was drawn by a steam engine which was fired with wood. We seemed to be going only about ten miles an hour. We reached Nakuru at about 7:00 P.M. where the train stopped about an hour for the passengers to eat supper at a nearby restaurant. Then on and on we went arriving at Kisumu at 5:20 the next morning. Brother Calvin Brallier was at the depot to meet us and take us to the mission station at Kima.

We were entertained that day by the missionaries and were given quarters in the Big House where we remained temporarily while we prepared to move into the house used by the Donohews.

It was perhaps our first night at Kima that we saw a large

African man stop and look at us through the window. He carried a spear and a club. We did not know what to think but afterwards learned he was a watchman sent to protect us. Really there was little danger except from thieves. There were several large dogs also on the mission which helped to keep order.

The next day we went to Kisumu where I secured a driver's license and a radio license, (permission to listen to a radio), to buy food and other small items.

Our first religious service was in the large Kima church Sunday morning at 7:30. I spoke on Eph. 2:8. In the afternoon we attended a convention at the Friend's mission where I spoke on Rom. 8:35-39. After a meal of obosuma (at that place it was called obosuka) we hurried home to avoid the rain. That night the staff had meeting at the LaFont residence where I spoke briefly again.

A day by day report of what occurred at the Kenya mission while we were there would be tedious and uninteresting. I shall deal in general matters with an occasional personal reference.

We found the Church of God in Nyanza Province consisting of 125 congregations. Some of these were small and some very large. Each church had its pastor and most of them conducted a school. The pastor might be both pastor and teacher though he himself had not gone beyond the third grade.

In addition to these local pastors there was a body of 20 to 24 elders who had been well trained by the missionaries. These elders exercised an oversight over the congregations and pastors, each elder having charge of 2 to 10 churches. These were well-established, faithful men who cared well for the flock.

Each congregation had its own church building, some very small mud buildings with thatched roofs and some large stone or brick buildings with metal roofs such as would do credit to some of the congregations in America. We were told that one of these buildings would hold 900 people (not seat them as it had no seats).

The largest and best building was at Kima and was called by

154

some, "The Cathedral in the Jungle." It was said to seat two or 3,000. (It had backless benches). Even so it would not always hold the crowds that came to meetings there. In addition to these churches that belonged to the African church the Missionary Board erected schools, hospitals and residences for its missionaries. On Sundays the missionaries would visit various congregations, usually going two by two, where they would preach and conduct Sunday school. Even so it would take a long time to visit all the churches. They were very busy during the week teaching, training, nursing, building and otherwise advancing the work always with the spiritual needs of the people chiefly in view. There were 16 adults in all.

The missionaries with the elders planned a series of meetings to be held in many of the churches. These were short meetings from Friday through Sunday. An elder would be in charge and would hold the meeting but at the last service, Sunday morning, a missionary would speak. I was sent to the meeting at Ebushangoli for the last service. Upon arriving I asked the elder how successful the meeting had been. He replied that 199 had been at the altar. At the morning service 63 others came making a total of 262. Of course not all of these were directly from heathenism for many had been under Christian influence and some were "warmed over". Other elders reported similar results.

These new converts were now required to attend baptismal classes where they would be taught Christian principles of living. These classes would continue weeks or months.

To be eligible for baptism one must be approved by his pastor or some responsible person. At a meeting of the pastors and leaders the elder would read the names of candidates. When a name was read, after a brief pause, the pastor teacher would arise and say, "Umyala," which means, "He is able," or "O. K." He is approved. But after the reading of one name there was a prolonged silence till someone arose and said, "He quarrels with his wife." He is rejected and must go back to baptismal classes. One woman was rejected for attending a theater in Nairobi.

Another man was rejected for playing his guitar. This surprised me till I learned he played it for a heathen dance.

A baptismal service was held at Kima at which 365 were baptised. A few days later 446 were baptised at Mwihila and 167 at Ingotse. At Ibeno, in the Kisii district, 20 were baptised, among them a young woman who had walked 48 miles to attend the meeting.

These baptismal services were usually followed by a communion service in which hundreds would take part. It was quite a sight to witness and quite a privilege to serve communion to people whose parents, if not they themselves, were born in heathenism.

An interesting event occurred in connection with the baptism at Mwihila which was conducted in the Yala River about a mile from the mission station. Among those baptised was a pregnant woman. On her way back to the mission she could wait no longer so stopped in the bushes by the side of the road and gave birth to a son. I thought an appropriate name would be "John the Baptist." I hear that is his name. I have heard of a priest baptising a child soon after birth but this one was baptised just before birth.

The British Government in Kenya showed its concern for the education of the African people by giving financial help and oversight of about 100 schools in the area about our mission. The government appointed one of our missionaries, Calvin Brallier, to supervise this work. This was a big job and a big opportunity for this gave him direct contact with teachers and students. He used this opportunity to organize youth work and to plan conventions for youth. Many young people were converted and very splendid leaders were found among the teachers.

Mention should be made of the girls' school at Kima which enrolled about 150 girls. This residence school, operated by Margaret LaFont was recognized as one of the best of its kind in the whole Colony. A similar boys' school was conducted at

Ingotse with a teacher-training school at Mwihila. There were other good schools.

At Kima there was a maternity hospital and a general hospital with 25 beds. Elsewhere there were clinics. These were conducted by nurses. All were looking eagerly for the arrival of Dr. Gaulke.

Although considerable progress had been made in education in general there remained one needy field. The well trained elders were filling their places well but they were getting along in years and there remained too great a gap between them and the regular pastors. There was need to evelate the entire group of ministers. The elders were not eager to relinquish their places of leadership, nor should they be, till others were better prepared to fill the gap.

Frank LaFont was doing a commendable work in teaching the elders and the younger ministers but the need for more training was clearly recognized. I conducted a number of classes with the elders with twenty-one in regular attendance. I wrote lessons in English which were translated for them. Also I addressed them and heard their questions through an interpretor.

But one of my concerns, and one thing the Board asked me to look into, was the need of a Bible training school for younger ministers. I thought one might be patterned somewhat after our American schools in their early stages with such adjustments as the situation might require.

Such a school might begin with a simple organization that would represent the African church, the mission and have the approval of the Board. The cost to begin with would be nominal. Appropriate buildings were available at Kima so that no great expense would be necessary. The Board should be responsible for the faculty but expense for food and incidentals should be borne by the students or by the congregation or clan from which they came.

I worked out a three years curriculum which could be extended to four years including the subjects most useful on preparing one for ministerial work and eventual places of leadership.

There would arise certain problems such as the selection of students and the placing and supporting of them when they would leave school. In view of the rapid changes in political and social affairs it would be impossible to solve all problems in advance. Some of them must be met as they occur.

Had I been footloose I should have been willing to attempt establishing such a school. I was asked to consider doing so but my connection with Pacific Bible College prevented me from doing so.

As Brother and Sister Donohew and Brother and Sister Schwieger were home on furlough and as Brother Donohew would be chiefly involved in starting such a school I decided to return home sooner than I had planned in order to confer with them and Brother Quinn concerning the plans I had worked out. But, as always happens at Anderson, there was practically no time to get together to discuss the plans I had worked out. However, at a later time, I discussed the matter with Brother Donohew and found his plans to be very much like mine.

A few days after we arrived in Kenya a newspaper headline screamed, "Six million Africans will massacre thirty thousand Europeans in one night." This fright grew out of the Mau Mau trouble which centered near Nairobi. It did not become very violent in our area though there were a few incidents of violence. One of them came near to us through a headman appointed by the chief. It came about this way.

In the early days of the mission when some were saved one or more of them would offer land on which to build a church. There were no deeds and no survey. It could happen that their unsaved children would later claim the land and demand it back. The Government instructed us to locate, measure and map the properties of the churches and have them gazetted. This was a very difficult task as none of the area had been surveyed and there were no established landmarks.

I purchased a compass and borrowed a tripod and constructed a crude surveying instrument. I made a disk having 360 degrees. By placing north at 0 and the pointer in the direction of the line I could learn the degrees of direction. Brother LaFont stepped off the distance. From the data thus secured I drew maps. We measured about 70 church plots in this fashion. An African brother helped us find the churches and learn the names.

The African chief knew what we were doing and approved of it. He appointed a headman to accompany us. This man had been associated with Brother Kramer in the early days and, though now backslid, pretended to be our friend. He would talk for us whenever one would try to reduce our area. But later this man was arrested as a spy for the Mau Mau. His papers included a list of prescribed persons which included my name and that of Frank LaFont. It is well that he was caught before the executioner caught up with us.

Our mission at Ibeno, 111 miles from our Kima station, was quite young. The people were clamoring for a missionary and a hospital or dispensary. We visited the chief to ask for land. He told us the land is not increasing but the population is. He should know for he had 15 wives and about 75 children. However he promised to have a headman "walk about" a place for us. We now have a mission there.

I am not conceited enough to think I accomplished a great amount while I was in Kenya. While I was there a few advances were made. The mission made some improvement in its bylaws. The Girl's School and the Teacher-Training School were approved to come under boards of governors which was in line with trends in the educational system and to advantage of our schools. The mission decided to join the Christian Council of Kenya (C.C.K.), the liaison group between the government and the missions.

The Missionary Board had asked me to assume the office of Secretary-Treasurer of the mission for the time I should be in Kenya. Shortly after my arrival Brother Brallier, who was acting temporarily, turned the office with the accounts and funds over to me. I instituted an improved system of handling the office in accord with the mission manual.

All tourists visiting Kenya are eager to see the wild animals in their natural habitat. I desired to do so and planned on five different times to make such a trip with Brother LaFont but each time I was prevented from going. I did not wish to shoot but only to see and take pictures. One time near Eldoret I saw a number of giraffes. As it is hard for them to get their heads to the ground they eat leaves and new sprouts from the tops of trees. Also I was privileged to visit the wild animal preserve near Niarobi where we saw many kinds of animals roaming loose. These included zebras, giraffes, wildebeasts, ostriches, wild hog, and lions. I missed seeing elephants and alligators.

It seemed strange to me that these animals roamed about without any evidence of fear, even of the lions. I learned that lions do not kill except for food and that this occurs only every four or five days. A night or two after we were there the lions went on a hunt. A lion will spring onto the back of its prey and with its powerful jaw sever the spine at the neck. This ends all struggle and all feeling. This seems a merciful way to kill even if the lion has no such intention.

If I were disposed to doubt the story of Daniel in the lion's den, which I am not, I would say it occurred on a day the lions were not eating but that Daniel's enemies were thrown in at meal time.

We had planned to return to Nairobi before starting on our homeward trip that we might buy some souvenirs, as such were not plentiful in Kisuma. But on account of the Mau Mau trouble near Nairobi we thought best not to go to Nairobi. Instead we took a small plane from Kisuma to Entebbe where we transferred to a BOAC plane for Cairo. We followed down the Nile much of the way. Our plane landed at Khartoum where it was very hot, 122°F. It was not quite so hot under shelter. That evening we landed at Cairo for another visit with the missionaries there, the Skaggses and Earnest LaFonts.

I shall ever hold in my memory the warm friends I met in Kenya. These are dear Christians and faithful ministers of Christ. The color of their skin seldom enters my mind. I preached in their churches and groves and dedicated some of their new buildings. I served as chairman of their ministerial assembly and advised with their leaders. They treated me with utmost respect. I visited in their homes and ate at their tables. I accepted offerings of chickens and eggs from them.

I think my deepest spiritual experience while there was in receiving the emblems of the communion at the hands of elders only one generation removed from heathenism. God has done a wonderful work among them.

When we were ready to leave the elders held a very impressive farewell service for us. They presented me with a briefcase and gave my wife a hand bag. Also they conferred on me the title of Omwami Omukhongo (Paramount Chief) and invested me with its insigna, a monkeyfur cape. This makes me (theoretically) chief over 16 other chiefs.

I hold sacred in my memory these dear brothers and sisters whose skins are black but whose hearts are white as snow.

The second day after returning to Cairo I accompanied Brothers Skaggs and LaFont on a trip up the Nile to visit some of our village churches. On our way we stopped at Memphis and saw the statue of Rameses II carved many centuries ago. We proceeded to Minia where we had services with the church of which Brother Shahata is pastor. He seemed to be a very capable man and well respected. We stayed overnight in a hotel in Minia.

The next day we went on to Mallowa and visited a village church. Here lazy gamoos stood around or soaked themselves in the ditch. Men and boys bathed in the raw and women washed their feet then took jugs of water home. One man carried water in a goat skin, like Bible times. I saw also a stack of grain with some spread out to be threshed by drawing a stoneboat over it by oxen. I prepared to take a picure when the oxen would come

161

into view dragging the stoneboat but instead it was drawn by a tractor! Here the old and the new had met.

We went on to Assuit where we met brethren and visited the American University and orphanage where care is given 750 children. From here we returned home and found it necessary to drive carefully for people on foot (and that means all of them) paid no attention to a car or its horn. They were there first and the road belongs to them.

On our return to Cairo we had a consultation with Brother Daoud concerning some problems. In a short time the problem was solved.

On Saturday nights the missionaries held a singspiration in English which was well attended by people interested in English. This was a good method of interesting new people. I spoke on Joy and the next morning spoke to the American congregation.

The great experience for which we had long waited was now before us—a visit to the Holy Land. On Monday morning we left Cairo by plane for Jerusalem via Bierut. Brothers Skaggs and LaFont were with us. From the air we could see the Suez Canal, Tyre, Port Said, Mt. Herman and the Lebanon and Antelebanan mountains. At Beirut we changed planes and flew to Jerusalem. On the way we saw the Sea of Galilee, the Jordan River and the Dead Sea. Upon our arrival at the Jerusalem airport we went to the American Colony Hotel. Brother Skaggs knew an Arab whom he hired to take us sightseeing. We were taken first to see the Church of the Holy Sepulcher, the reputed place of Christ's burial. There were none of the appearances of a tomb but a small room in which a monk stood receiving tips. Near by there was a stone slab on which it is said the body of Christ was prepared for burial. Worshippers were kneeling down and kissing this stone. This elegantly ornamented place did not impress us as being the actual place of the crucifixion and burial of Christ.

The next day we visited the Jordan Valley. On our way to Jericho we passed the supposed location of the inn to which the Samaritan brought the robbed man. There is an old building there, but not old enough to be the same inn. We also saw the Brook Cherith where Elijah was fed by the ravens. There were ravens flying about, probably the descendants of Elijah's ravens. The Mount of Temptation was pointed out to us from which Christ was shown the kingdoms of the world.

We found the Jordan River small by our standards and quite muddy. No wonder Naaman preferred the rivers of Damascus. We stood on the Allenby bridge and wondered where Christ was baptized and where Joshua crossed over. We looked also across to the land of Moab and speculated as to the point from which Moses viewed the land and where he was buried.

While in the Jordan Valley we visited the Dead Sea. This is the lowest spot on earth. The sea is rich in chemicals washed down into it by the Jordan and its tributaries. But it is void, or nearly so, of all marine life.

We passed the sight of Jericho where archeologists had been digging in the ruins. And we saw other ruins more dreadful, namely, 125,000 refugees living in small huts eking out a bare existence and depending on handouts. I saw them stand in line at an open window to receive a small package of food with nothing to look forward to except eventual death.

Returning from the Jordan Valley we visited the garden tomb. A short distance outside the north wall of Jerusalem stands Skull Hill, a perpendicular wall with caves that appear like eyes and a mouth. Many scholars believe this is the Golgotha of the Bible. There is no similar formation elsewhere near Jerusalem. In the side of this wall, not far away, a tomb has been carved out. We entered the tomb and examined it. Everything connected with this area is in agreement with the scriptural accounts of the crucifixion of Christ and his burial. It is preferred by many over the supposed location within the city.

After visiting the tomb we visited Gethsemane and entered the cave where we were told Christ prayed in agony while his disciples slept. If this tradition is true his prayer was not under an olive tree, as some suppose. There are very old olive trees nearby but it is not likely any of them are 2,000 years old.

We ascended to the top of the Mount of Olives where stands a small building indicating the spot from which Christ ascended. Here is a large footprint which it is supposed was left by him as he sprang from the earth. I saw only one footprint. I do not know where the other is unless at Rome.

We visited Bethany which is on the side of the Mount of Olives. The grave of Lazarus is here. And Luke tells us that it was from near Bethany that Christ ascended. He did not need to go to the top of the mountain to get a good start.

The next day we journeyed to Bethlehem. Here we could see the shepherds' pasture and visited the Church of the Nativity. Beneath the church is a small cave in which it is said Christ was born. The exact spot is marked with a star laid in the floor. A short distance away is the place of the manger where he was laid. Over this cave the large church is built with three divisions for the Catholics, the Orthodox and the Armenians. There is not much love between these factions. We were told the Catholics pass through the Armenian section on their way to the cave but the Armenians will not permit the Catholics to step on their carpet. Even at the Church of the Holy Sepulchar the Christian factions quarrel till Moslem Arabs must police the place to keep order.

We visited the Temple area. The Dome of the Rock, sometimes called, wrongly, the Mosque of Omar, occupies the most sacred place on earth. This is believed to be the place where Abraham offered up Isaac and it is where Solomon's brazen altar stood. Here, and here only, the Jews might offer sacrifices for sins but now no Jew is allowed on the premises. Nearby is a Mohammedan Mosque.

We traveled northward from Jerusalem to Sychar and drank from Jacob's well. (The water Christ gives is better.) The well is deep. There are Mt. Geribim and Mt. Ebal, Nabulus, Shechem, Sebastan and the ruins of Samaria, all visited by us. We sought to see the old Samaritan MS of the Pentateuch but the synagogue was closed as the people were worshipping on Mt. Gerizim that day. (See John 4:20). We could not visit Nazareth as our passport did not include Israel where Nazareth is located.

Having completed our tour of the Holy Land we returned to Beirut where we met Brother Ibriham Shada Maloof, one of our old missionaries who had labored with Brother Riggle. Brother Maloof had one son who was a doctor and another in public service. He had other noted children also. We visited in the home of one of them and found them to be very fine people. Brother Maloof was doing missionary work in a remote area of Syria.

We attended the evening service at the church and I was asked to speak. They have a nice building and a very responsive group of people. They have become an indigenous church with local leaders. This work was built up largely by the Croses.

Our plans included a trip to Damascus. On the way we visited the ruins of ancient Baalbeck. Here are high pillars that have stood for hundreds of years and other ruins now deserted.

We had secured a permit to enter Syria but when we reached the border we learned we did not have a prmit for reentry of Lebanon. If we went on in how would we get out again? Brother Skaggs was able to arrange for our reentry, so we proceeded to Damascus, reputed to be the oldest city with continuous inhabitation in the world. It was known by Abraham. (Gen. 15:2). The city is attractive. It is said that Mohammed refused to enter Damascus saying he did not wish to enter Paradise twice.

We were unable to locate the place where Paul was smitten with blindness but we entered the city through the same gate by which he entered at the end of the "street called straight." Just inside the gate a small chapel marks the location of the home of Ananias who visited Paul. We traveled the full length of this street so must have passed the site of the "house of Judas," but the house is no longer there. This is where Paul received his sight.

We were shown the gate where Paul was let down in a basket but we doubt this was the true place for all gates were watched closely lest Paul escape.

Flowing through the city is a stream of clear water to which Naaman referred when he objected to bathing in the muddy Jordan.

After our visit to Damascus we returned to Beirut where Brother Skaggs and Brother LaFont left us. From this point my wife and I were on our own. First we flew to Athens. Here we were entertained by James Zazanis who escorted us over the city to see ancient places of interest. We visited the acropolis and Mars Hill. I stood, so I was told, on the very spot where Paul stood as he addressed the philosophers (Acts 17). If it was not the exact spot at least it was near.

We attended our Sunday night service at which I was asked to speak. A goodly crowd of intelligent people were present. The service was held in a hall but I was shown the lot which has since been covered with a new church building.

The next day Brother Zazanis took us to the old city of Corinth where we viewed ancient ruins. For a year and a half Paul preached in this city. Near the city an isthmus is cut by the Corinth Canal shortening the distance to Athens from the west. We saw little signs of vital Christianity. The scenery along the sea between Athens and Corinth is very beautiful.

From Athens we flew to Rome. We had not made reservations but secured a room at the Marconi hotel. The next day we took a sight-seeing tour visiting an art gallery, the Pantheon and Saint Peter's Cathedral, said to be the largest church in the world (although Saint Catherine's Cathedral in Constantinople, which is no longer a Christian church, may be larger).

Within Saint Peter's was a large crowd of worshippers and sightseers. It was interesting to watch the crowd gather around the brass statue of Saint Peter. Here worshipper after worshipper would walk up and kiss his big toe. One lady, who appeared to be smart, wiped the toe with her handkerchief before kissing it. Another just threw a kiss with her hand. People were bowing in prayer before images. We might look down stairs to the place where Peter's bones were found but we were not permitted to go down.

I have been asked whether I saw the pope. I did not. I was not eager for, as I explain, I have seen many sinners. But perhaps we should have met for it might do him good to see a real live saint in the flesh. His saints are all dead.

After the tour I walked around a bit. I visited the Colosseum with part of its walls still standing. Here many true saints sealed their lives with their blood. I did not see the holy stairs up which Luther climbed on his knees. There was much to see that I missed. One needs much time to see a city such as Rome.

Our next stop was to be Milano. We took the electric train from Rome to Milano passing over the Appennine Mountains. It was interesting to see the many large grape vinyards with their well-kept vines. We reached Milano in the afternoon. I left my wife at the depot as it was raining while I looked for a hotel. I found one near by where we secured a room. I wanted so much to see the Milan Cathedral which was centuries in building, but we were delayed and the next morning there was not sufficient time before our train would leave. So we paid our hotel bill and took the train for Zurich, Switzerland. It was a beautiful trip through the Alps where the mountains were high with beautiful valleys between, some narrow, some broad, but all very beautiful, a land of peace and prosperity.

We reached Zurich at about five in the evening and were met by Brother and Sister Zuber who took us to their home. Brother Zuber could speak some English and their daughter spoke quite well but Sister Zuber knew no English. It was interesting to hear her and Mrs. Gray talk together when neither could understand what the other was saying.

Zurich is a beautiful city on the shore of a beautiful lake, surrounded by high mountains. Everywhere were the marks of prosperity and peace. Switzerland seemed to me the most prosperous country in Europe that we saw. It had succeeded in keeping out of other people's wars.

On Sunday we accompanied Brother Zuber to Basil where a meeting for workers was being held. I was privileged to speak to them. We returned to Zurich that evening.

There are places of historic interest in Zurich. The one that interested me most was the church where Ulrich Zwingli carried on his work of reformation. His influence was not quite so wide as that of Luther but his message was similar and even clearer.

I was in Zurich over Ascension Day which, in Switzerland, is a holiday. Church services are held on that day. It was my pleasure to speak to our church group. Brother Kersten interpreted for me.

Before leaving Kenya I wrote Brother Quinn that I had enough funds to reach Zurich and asked him to send me $300 for the rest of the trip. It seems he did not receive my letter for no funds were sent. After waiting a few days I cabled him for funds. This delay caused us to stay in Zurich longer than we had planned but we enjoyed our stay there very much. Brother and Sister Zuber were fine Christian friends. After receiving our funds we prepared to leave for Fritzlar, Germany, our next stop.

On our way from Zurich to Fritzlar we changed cars at Basil, Karlsruhe, Frankfort and Wabern reaching Fritzlar at night. The next day being Sunday I spoke at the 10:00 A.M. service. That night I spoke at Kassel, where we had gone to visit, returning to Fritzlar that night. Fritzlar is a very old city with some very old buildings still standing. I was told that a German Emperor was crowned here about 1,000 years ago. It was here that our brethren have erected a Bible school for the training of ministers. It offers a four years course. I found fourteen students in attendance. I spent much of Monday and Tuesday addressing the students on doctrinal subjects.

On Wednesday we left Fritzlar for Essen. That being prayer-meeting night I spoke to the congregation. In the next few days I went with Brother Klabunde to see some new churches under construction and saw one place that reminded me of Bethlehem; the congregation was using a stable as a place of worship.

Sunday morning I spoke again at Essen and then in the afternoon at Dinslacken and visited with Brother Waurich, the pastor, whose daughter had been a student at Pacific Bible College but was now assisting at the school at Fritzlar.

On Monday we went to Bochum and visited Brother Malcon and also to Wattenscheid where we met the parents of the Naumanns who had come to Portland to attend the College. Here we met Brother Begemann and addressed his congregation. On Tuesday a ministers meeting was held at Wattenscheid which was attended by Brothers Waurich of Dinslagen, Begemann of Wattenscheid, Malcon of Bochun, Killisch of Hamborn, Klabunde of Essen, and one or two others.

The next day we continued our journey toward London. Our train passed across Holland to Hook of Holland where we took a boat to cross the North Sea to Harwick, England.

At Hook of Holland our passports were examined and we had no difficulty getting through customs. But when we went on board we found that all bunks were taken so we, and about 50 others, sat up all night. We sat at tables with our heads resting on pillows. It was a long night and we were glad to reach Harwick in the morning. We had no difficulty passing through immigration and customs and were soon on our train speeding toward London.

Upon our arrival in London we took a taxi to the Rest Home at 10 Finchley Road, St. John's Wood, N. W. 8, where we had made reservations. This is a home for missionaries going to or coming from their fields. It is an old mansion operated economically with small cost to its patrons. As food was then rationed in England the meals were frugal. At our first dinner we had for entree a boiled onion. Downtown restaurants offered scant menus.

Among the missionaries at the Home we found a few that knew a little about our mission but there was only one person that I knew. He was Gus Jeeninga.

We did not see as much of London as we had hoped to see

as our stay was limited and the weather was unfavorable. On our first day I walked over a part of the city and visited Hyde Park. On the next day we took the bus to down town and visited several places of interest. We learned of a tour which would take us over the route of the Queen's coronation. We took the tour which was lined much of the way with bleachers and bunting. Here many thousands of people would see the queen ride by. Her coronation was the main topic of conversation, even among the missionaries. We were urged to stay to see the parade but we had already made our flight reservations. But instead of sitting on a bleacher to watch the parade we were in it! We rode in a car ahead of the Queen's car (4 days ahead)!!

Saturday was a rainy day not suited for sightseeing so we stayed in most of the day. Really one needs a week or more to see London. So on Sunday forenoon we had a taxi take us to the BOAC office where we had our tickets validated and our baggage checked. At 1:15 we were taken to the airport where we were placed on board our plane for New York.

Our plane stopped first at a field near Glasgow, Scotland. This was interesting to me as I understand I have ancestors who were Scotch. I alighted from the plane and walked on the soil of old Scotland.

Our next stop was at Gander, Newfoundland. After a short stop we proceeded to New York where we arrived at 4:30 A.M. New York time.

We remained in New York a few days staying at the Missionary Home, 2132 Grand Avenue. On Tuesday, June 2, we visited Brother Wampler and were able to see on television the Queen's procession and also her coronation within the cathedral which is much more than could be seen from the choicest bleacher seat in London.

When we were prepared to leave for Anderson we decided to take the New York Central train up the Hudson river. I had been in New York before but had not taken this route. We went through Albany and Buffalo and reached Anderson the next morning.

We remained in Anderson through the campmeeting till the last Saturday when we rode with Brother Jaynes to his home at Whitmire, S. C. where we remained over Sunday. I spoke in the morning and showed African pictures at night. Through the aid of Brother Jaynes I purchased a new Chrysler for $2,400.00 and on Monday started on our way to Portland. Along the way we stopped at Tallapoosa, Ga., Conway, Ark., Clay Center, Kas., Cheyenne, Wyo., Twin Falls, Ida., and on to Portland, a total of 3,200 miles. At home again.

APPENDIX NO. 1
My Literary Work

Over a period of forty years I wrote scores and scores of articles for the Gospel Trumpet. With three or four exceptions all of these were published. Usually I wrote as the inspiration came but sometimes on request. I have written some for other magazines.

After coming into contact with Mormon people I wrote my first book, The Menace of Mormonism, pulished in 1926. I first studied Mormon literature then answered them with the Bible.

In the same year I prepared a series of four quarterlies for Sunday School use at the request of the Gospel Trumpet Company. Later these were replaced with a series of two quarterlies based somewhat on my Christian Theology. These were doctrinal quarterlies.

At the request of the Gospel Trumpet Company I wrote two volumes on Christian Theology. The first volume was published in 1944 and the second in 1946. Later the two were combined into one volume. The book is arranged in six parts making it suitable for use as a text book on either the semester or the quarterly plan. It has been used by different colleges and has been translated, at least in part.

In 1950 I wrote a book called How To Study The Bible. It was used for a time as a text for a Christian Education course.

In 1960 another book of mine was published by the Warner Press. It is entitled, The Nature of the Church. This book traces the development of the church through the ages pointing out the causes of division and pointing a simple way to Christian unity.

Some years ago I began to collect material for another book but laid this aside to write my biography. Now that this task is about finished with little left to write but an obituary (which I cannot write yet) I may return to this book.

Poetry and Music

As a young man I wrote a number of poems which were unworthy of the name as they were little more than prose put to meter. Later I wrote a few that have some merit. One of these was a poem entitled, Speak To My Heart. It was published in the Gospel Trumpet and I wrote music for it in the form of a ladies' trio. This is my favorite, and when sung well it is very moving.

One day while driving alone from Walla Walla to Clarkston there came running through my mind these words, "Sometimes my eyes are tearful; sometimes my heart is sad." There came a tune along with the words. The words and music grew into a song entitled, Jesus Is Near. I completed the song, wrote the music and harmonized it.

I wrote two numbers of a different kind. They were intended for choir use. One was a Palm Sunday number entitled Hosanna. The other was an Easter number called, Christ Is Risen. Both have been sung by choirs with good effect.

I began another number with a Christmas setting but have not finished it. There is so much good Christmas music there seems little call for anything more I might write. However I may complete it for the pleasure it can give me to do so.

The music for my songs I have written and harmonized myself except our College Alma Mater the tune of which is borrowed from Cornell. I wrote it out by ear and harmonized it.

172

My latest poem is entitled, An Ode To Death. I wrote this while my wife, Rosa, lay in the mortuary. The poem was read at her funeral that day.

I have written another poem called Man's Master as a sequal to a poem written by E. G. Masters entitled, Styles.

Whether I will ever write more I cannot tell.

APPENDIX NO. 2
POSITIONS I HAVE HELD

There are few persons in the church who have held as many or more offices than I have held. I have never sought an office and have never asked anyone to vote for me. Only once did I vote for myself. That was for a place I thought God wanted me to have. I felt so ashamed for thinking God needed my help to give me the place that I never again voted for myself.

I have been on each of our national boards except the Board of Christian Education and the Board of Pensions. Once I was nominated for the Christian Education board and lost by three votes. I was glad for I knew the other man was well qualified for the position, more so than I.

The positions here listed do not include those of a local nature, such as trustee or treasurer of a local church or some lesser postion of a temporary nature, such as a nominating body. The list is not entirely complete but to the best of my knowledge is correct.

The earliest organized committee of which I am aware was set up at the midwinter assembly at Spokane in 1913-1914. It was to serve this annual assembly and the Colfax campmeeting. Its purpose was to control the pulpit. Heretofore there was no program and each preacher preached as he felt he had a message. This worked fairly well till a young fellow took the pulpit and made a mess of things. This committee was not to dictate but yielded the pulpit to any who asked unless there was a definite reason to refuse. If two asked for the same service they were

173

instructed to settle between them in prayer which should preach. It might happen that no one would apply in which case the committee might need to seek someone. The committee elected consisted of, G. W. Bailey, chairman, A. F. Gray, secretary and C. H. Fly, treasurer (though we handled no money).

In about the year 1915 there was organized the Presbytery of the Church of God of the Inland Empire. The office of District Overseer was created and Brother G. W. Bailey was elected to that office. I was elected secretary.

At the Anderson campmeeting in 1919 Brother F. G. Smith preached a strong message on "Charismatic Church Government." After the service Brother Bailey said to me, "I think we had better back up." I replied, "I think we had." So at the Colfax campmeeting the office of District Overseer was abolished. The office of chairman was restored and I was retained as secretary.

For forty years my name appeared on each issue of the *Gospel Trumpet* as a staff contributor or member of the publication committee. During this time I contributed many articles to the Gospel Trumpet, mostly doctrinal. Also I wrote tracts and Sunday School lessons. Besides my Christian Theology, which appeared in two volumes, I have written three other books. I have written a few tracts and a few songs, words and music, and a little poetry.

I served two years as Vice Chairman and seventeen as Chairman of the General Ministerial Assembly.

During my ministry I have preached in more than 300 places in half of the States and in ten foreign countries.

My brethren have thrust upon me many honors that I have neither sought nor deserved. I am well aware that of whatever value my life has been is only by the grace of God.

When this writing reaches the public I will have reached my four score years. I hope to render some more service while waiting for Gabriel to call me and the tide "turns again home."

Inland Empire Committees on which I served

Secretary, Devotional Committee, 1914-
Secretary, Ministerial Association, 1915-

Secretary, Presbytery, 1916-1919
Secretary, Inland Empire Missionary Board, 1915-1925
Treasurer, Inland Empire Missionary Board, 1919-1925
Delegate to Anderson General Assembly, 1918

State of Washington

Member, Washington Evangelistic Board, 1923-
State Secretary, Board of Church Extension, 1934-1938
State Secretary, Missionary Board, 1934-1938
State Secretary, Anderson College 1934-1938

Western Washington

Chairman, Western Washington Ministerial Association, 1933-1938
Member, Puget Sound Missionary Board, 1933-1938
President, Puget Sound Missionary Board, 1933-1938

Southern Idaho

Secretary, Campmeeting Association, 1921-1922

Oregon

Chairman, Association of the Churches of God in Oregon (2 years)
Member, Credentials and Advisory Board
Chairman, Evangelistic Committee

Indiana

Chairman, Indiana Ministerial Assembly, 1929, 1933
Member, Complaints Committee, 1930, 1932
Member, Executive Committee, 1932-1933
Member, Radio Committee, 1932-1933
Chairman, Executive Committee, 1932-1933
Chairman, Complaints Committee, 1932
Chairman, Radio Committee, 1932-1933

Central Indiana

Chairman, Ministerial Association

Northwest Ministerial Assembly

Chairman, 1922, 1934, 1935
Member, Board of Trustees, P. B. I., 1919-1923
President, Board of Trustees, P. B. I., 1919-1923
Principal, P. B. I., 1920-1923
Delegate to Anderson Assembly, 1919

General Boards

Member, Board of Church Extension, 1920-1921
Member, Missionary Board, 1924-1959
Member, Board of Trustees, Anderson College, 1925-1946
Member, Gospel Trumpet Company, 1933-1954

Member, Executive Council, 1932-1953
Member, Executive Committee, Anderson College, 1926-1933
Member, Executive Committee, Mission Board, 1927-1933
Member, Executive Committee, Board of Church Extension, 1931-1933
President, Missionary Board, 1927-1933
Vice-President, Anderson College, 1931-1934
Chairman, Anderson College Trustees, 1931-1945
Vice-Chairman, Ministerial Assembly, 1933-1934
Chairman, Ministerial Assembly, 1935-1936, 1939-1954
Member, Publication Committee, Gospel Trumpet Co., 1922-1962
Staff Contributor, Gospel Trumpet, 1922-1962
(I moved from Anderson in 1933 which brought several offices to end.)
I have served the General Ministerial Assembly as Chairman of its Business
Committee and its parliamentarian. I have served on World Service and the
Commission on Revision and Planning (but not on its Interim Committee.)
I have served also on the Program Committee of the Anderson Campmeeting.

Pacific Bible College (Warner Pacific College)

Member, Board of Trustees, 1937-1957
President, 1937-1957
Member of Executive Committee, 1957-1960
Member of Faculty, 1937-1960, 1963-
    None of these positions was salaried except when serving Pacific Bible
Institute and Pacific Bible College.
    I taught for Anderson College one year, 1929-1930, on an exchange
basis, one of its teachers assisting me in pastoral work.

Inter-Church Relations

Secretary, Lewiston-Clarkston Ministerial Association, 1916-1917
President, Lewiston-Clarkston Ministerial Association, 1917-1918
Vice-President, Anderson Ministerial Association, 1927-1928
President, Anderson Ministerial Association, 1928-1929
Note: We opened our church work in Clarkston in a vacant hotel. We felt
very insignificant. The pastor of the Christian Church, the largest in the city,
made himself known to me and invited me to go with him to the ministers
meeting. I had been taught not to mix with sectarians, but he was so kind
I could not refuse him so I went. At the meeting he introduced me and I
was voted into membership before I had time to speak. But I knew they
could not force me to attend. I was given equal privileges to speak. I found
they were sincere men serving God as best they knew. I have found the
same situation in other places.

Outside Relations

Member, Near East Relief Committee
Member, China Relief Committee
Member (honorary), Mark Twain Society of Authors

Note: All I have recited is of little importance. Once I asked Dr. Monk,
"When I was ordained do you suppose the angel in heaven got down the

big white book and wrote 'Rev.' in front of my name? or when I received my degree he took down the book and wrote after my name 'D. D.'? He replied, "I think not." When the roll is called up yonder I hope only to answer, "Saved through Jesus' blood." Nothing else will matter then.

APPENDIX NO. 3

The following is a list of places where I have spoken. The list includes places of a single service, or perhaps a wedding or a funeral, and those of extended or repeated protracted meetings including pastorates. The list may contain some errors and is not complete for I do not have the names of all places where I have spoken. Including these the list runs well over 300.

Alaska
Juneau

California
Arlington
Bakersfield
Chico
Exeter
Fresno
Hanford
Long Beach
   College Pk.
   Willow St.
Los Angeles
   First
   Highland Pk.
   East L. A.
Maders
Modesto
Oakland
Pacific Palisades
Parlier
Pasadena
Pomona
Redding
Reedley
Richmond
Sacramento
San Bernardino
San Diego
San Francisco
San Jose
Santa Cruz
   Advent camp
   Nazarene camp

First
   Community
Stockton
Tulare
Vallejo
Whittier

Colorado
Delta
Denver
N. Denver
Palmer Lake C. M.

Georgia
Atlanta

Idaho
Ahsahka
American Ridge
Arrow
Bethel
Beulah
Boise
Cavendish
Chesley
Clearwater
Coeur d'Alene
Cottonwood Crk.
Cream Ridge
Corrin's
Culdesac
Deer Flat
Craigmont
Evans School
Fairburn
Ford's Mill
Fraser

Genesee
Grangeville
Harpster
Howard's
Huston
Ilo
Johnson's
Juliaetta
Kamiah
Kidder Ridge
Kippen
Leland
Lenore
Lewiston
Melrose
Middleton
Midvale
Mohler
Myrtle
Moscow
Nex Perce
Nora
Orofino
Payette
Peck
Pine City
Pippenger School
Post Falls
Palouse River
Ramey's Mill
Randall Flat
Reubens
Pleasant Valley
Sandpoint
Southwick

177

Spalding
Stites
Tammany School
Taylor's
Troy
Viola
Twin Falls
Webb
Whiskey Creek
Winchester

Illinois
Bloomington
McLean
Rantoon
W. Frankfort

Indiana
Anderson
  Arrow Heights
  Jackson Park
  Meridian
  Park Place
  N. Anderson
Bethel
Bedford
Elwood
Fort Wayne
Huntington
Indianapolis
Lake Bethel
Marion
Muncie
New Albany
South Bend
Woodville
Yellow Lake C. M.

Iowa
Barney

Kentucky
Louisville

Maryland
Baltimore

Massachusetts
Conway Camp

Michigan
Grand Junction C. M.

Minnesota
Minneapolis
Saint Paul

Missouri
Kansas City

Montana
Billings
Crow Agency
Eureka
Hardin
Libby

Nebraska
Hastings

New York
New York City
  Grand Ave.
  Jamaica
  Williamsbridge
Niagara Falls

North Dakota
Erie
Grand Forks
Grand Forks C. M.

Ohio
Dayton (King)
Dayton (Sterner)
Piqua
Springfield C. M.

Oregon
Albany
Aloha
Ashland
Baker
Bandon
Bend
Clackamas C. M.
Corvallis
Estacada
Eugene
Gales Creek
Grants Pass
Hood River
Kelso
Klamath Falls
LaGrande
Lebanon
Medford
Milton-Freewater
Nelscott
Newberg
Milwaukie
  Ardenwald

North Bend
Oak Ridge
Oregon City
Portland
  Alameda
  Holladay Park
  Irving Park
  Lents-Gilbert
  Linchwood
  Metropolitan
  Richmond
  Rockwood
  Sellwood Park
  Trinity
  Trinity Baptist
  United Brethren
  Woodstock
Rainier
Roseburg
St. Helens
Scio
Woodburn

South Carolina
Whitmire

South Dakota
Brookings
Sioux Falls

Tennessee
Ashland City
Memphis

Utah
Salt Lake City

Washington
Aberdeen
Addy
Albion
Algona
Almota
Asotin
Bellingham
Burbank
Burlington
Camas
Centralia
Clarkston
Colfax
Deer Park
Edmonds
Edmonds C. M.

178

Egypt
Elma
Everett
Grandview
Hillyard
Jerry
Kelse
Kennewick
Lake Retreat
Lake Serene
Longview
Montesano
Olson's
Olympia
Onolaska
Orting
Parkland
Palouse
Pasco
Peach
Penruth
Puyallup
Renton
Rock Springs
Saints Home C. M.
Seattle
  Bow Lake
  South Park
  Woodland Park
Spanaway
Spokane
  Ash & Chelan
  Ash & Dean
  Lincoln Street

Sunnyside
Tekoa
Tulalip
Vancouver
Vineland
Walla Walla
Wenatchee
Yakima
Zilla

Wisconsin
Milwaukee
  D. C.
Washington
  (Colored)
  Martin's
  Memorial
  Wisconsin Ave.

Canada
Alberta
Camrose
Edmonton
Provost

Ontario
London

Saskatchewan
Saskatoon

Egypt
Cairo
  Armenian
  Egyptian
  English
  Greek

Minia
  Greece
Athens
  Lebanon
Beirut
  Japan
Tokyo
  Five or six churches
  Two 50 miles distant
  Kenya
Ibeno
Ingotse
Kima
Maseno
Mwhila
Nairobi
  Many local churches
  Korea
Heijo (Pyongyang)
Keijo (Seoul)
  Philippines
Laoag
  Germany
Dinslaken
Essen
Fritzlar
Kassel
Wattenscheid
  Switzerland
Basil
Zurich

Albert & Rosa
1927

Albert & Anna
1962